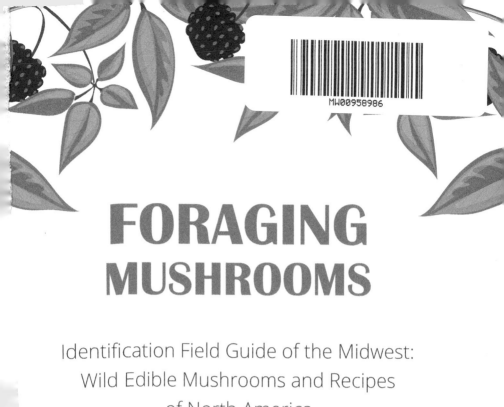

FORAGING MUSHROOMS

Identification Field Guide of the Midwest:
Wild Edible Mushrooms and Recipes
of North America

BLEU SAYLES

www.bleusayles.com

Table of Content

HERE IS A SPECIAL GIFT TO OUR READERS
Included with your purchase of this book is our 7 Expert
Rules to Foraging: A Journey to Becoming A Pro

This guide will help you prepare for your next adventure
whether it's in the wild or your own backyard.

Scan QR code below and provide us with an email for
delivery.

Chapter 1:

Mushroom Foraging in the Midwest

When looking at the Midwestern states, or the "flyover states," from the air, you might only notice the vast swaths of cultivated fields, wide-open prairies, and stretching forests. In fact, in the popular consciousness, this part of the United States is generally characterized by a sense of largeness: expansive fields, a boundless sky, and enormous rivers. But when you take a closer look, you'll be able to see that the large, varied landscapes of the Midwest are filled with tiny, hidden mushrooms ready to be hunted and harvested by intrepid fungi foragers!

The Midwest region consists of twelve states that sit right in the middle of the United States, thus its other nickname, "the heartland." These states are North and South Dakota, Kansas, Minne-sota, Iowa, Missouri, Wisconsin, Illinois, Indiana, Michigan, and Ohio. While located in the same region, they are vastly different in terms of habitats, meaning that mushroom foragers can have their pick of locations in which to uncover delicious mushrooms.

No matter if you are a beginner or expert mushroom forager, there are plenty of mushrooms for you to discover in the Midwest, from the far-reaching forests of the Black Hills to the gentle hills of the Ozarks to the banks of the Great Lakes.

Foraging in Midwestern Forests

In the stunning green national forests and smaller wooded areas that spread across millions of acres in the Midwest, you can find a plethora of mushrooms that grow on or form relationships with the various trees and plants in this habitat. Some mushrooms, known as parasitic mushrooms, grow directly on and get their nutrients from living tree trunks, while others, called saprotrophic mushrooms, feed on the dead matter of dying or decaying trees or logs. Yet other mushrooms, mycorrhizal mushrooms, form a give-and-take relationship with trees and plants, growing among tree roots on the forest floor.

Different mushrooms also prefer to grow on or near other trees. To find the mushroom you want to forage, you can look in forest habitats filled with the kind of tree that mushrooms like best, from the hardwood Shawnee National Forest in southern Illinois to the pine-filled Black Hills National Forest in Wyoming and South Dakota.

Some of the bountiful edible mushrooms you can find in these Midwest forests are crown-tipped coral mushrooms sprouting from fallen trees or buried logs, jelly-like wood ears growing on hickory trees, or winter chanterelles buried around the roots of oaks and other hardwood trees. If you want to forage for mushrooms, you can't go wrong by looking in Midwestern forests!

Plains and Prairies

If you think about the Midwest region, the first type of habitat that comes to your mind might be the grasslands—the far-reaching plains and rolling grasslands stretching to the horizon. The Great Plains and other prairie lands stretch across almost all of the Midwest.

These prairies are not homogenous, however. They are almost as varied as the wild, edible mushrooms they offer. In the Midwest, you can find sandy or hilly prairies with scrubby weeds, oak savannas covered by green ground cover and shady trees, and vast green and brown grasslands dotted by colorful prairie flowers.

Many mushrooms grow alongside these trees and plants or sprout from the grassy fields, like the white meadow mushrooms and horse mushrooms growing in fairy rings or arcs across the grasses.

Any forager should take the time to wander the hills and fields that cover most of the Midwest!

Midwestern Wetlands and Waterways

While the wetlands and waterways of the Midwest are an important part of the region, they're not prime hunting grounds for mushroom foragers. Some mushrooms, such as much-coveted morels, do grow in the Great Lakes region, but you'll be hard-pressed to find mushrooms growing in bogs, swamps, riverbeds, or lakeshores. Most fruiting, edible mushroom bodies need a certain amount of dryness to flourish.

Heartland Highlands: Appalachia and the Ozarks

The Ozarks is a mountainous highland stretching across Missouri in the south part of the Midwest. This heartland highland possesses edible mushrooms that thrive on its rolling hills and stretches of grassy plains, inside its sprawling forests, and on its many riverbanks.

Due to its wide variety of habitats in close quarters, the Ozarks is a great place for any forager to spend time. You can find unique, yellow chicken fat mushrooms in the lower elevations of the Ozarks.

While the Ozarks is the highland that dominates the southern Midwest, one piece of the ancient Appalachian Mountains passes through Ohio in the eastern region. This mountain range has a rich history of foraging, reaching back thousands of years.

The intrepid Midwestern hiker can find the stooped, shaggy mushroom known as man of the woods hiding deep in Appalachia. Beginners can stick to the popular walking trails, while experienced hikers and forgers can venture deeper into these ancient highland forests!

Urban Areas

For some mushrooms, you won't need to venture far into the wild. Populated parks, lawns, backyards, and walking trails scattered across the Midwest can host a variety of edible fungi. Some mushrooms crop up in private gardens and yards, especially where wood chips are laid down. For instance, some of these urban mushrooms—the elegant stinkhorn and orange peel mushroom—are perfectly edible.

Foraging Laws

Many Midwestern states are proud of their foraging heritage, and all across the region, you can find support and education for foragers. Many states have their own mycological clubs or societies that welcome newcomers, and these local experts can help you determine the laws in your area.

Whether or not you're part of a larger foraging group, you need to double-check the foraging laws that apply to that state or area when you plan a foraging trip. For instance, in Illinois county, which contains Chicago, mushroom foragers can forage in state parks but not in forest preserves (O'Connor, 2017).

While state and federal lands, like National Parks, generally welcome private foragers, county or local parks might have stricter rules for who can and cannot forage. Check if you need any kind of permit before you head out into your foraging habitat.

Seasons in the Edible, Wild Heartland

The offerings of these Midwestern landscapes range from season to season. Since each season in this region is distinct, the mushrooms available change based on humidity and temperature.

Especially in the north, the winters deliver heavy snows that melt to reveal hidden mushrooms; spring means mushrooms appear in high numbers after heavy rains; summer brings soaring temperatures that draw out the more hardy mushrooms, and autumn's cool weather calls out dozens of colorful mushroom that thrive until the first frosts of winter.

Be aware of how the changing seasons affect each habitat. In the winter woods, you can be sure to find wood ears and winter chanterelles ripe for the picking; beside spring creeks, you can search for black trumpet mushrooms. Use the chapters of this book as a basic guide for which edible fungi are available during the different seasons.

So get your gear, find a friend, and head out into the wild places to uncover the treasure troves of wild, edible mushrooms that can be found in America's heartland!

Chapter 2:

An Introduction to Mycology and Mushroom Foraging

Every day, thousands of people all over the world hike through wooded and urban areas in quest of the ultimate edible plant: mushrooms. These foragers share a love of delicious, wild, edible fungi that, once cooked, become a delicious, nutritious, fragrant food that's a delight to bite into. Whether mushroom hunters forage alone or with a group, in the wilderness or city parks, or as beginners or seasoned foragers, each of these people has found a hobby that is not only fun but is also spiritually, culinarily, and physically fulfilling.

I was one such person. Growing up in Boulder, Colorado, my father would often take me on long hikes through the breathtaking parks and trails. On these hikes, I discovered a love for the wild plants that grew in these places. I was in awe of the diversity I saw around me and how valuable these plants could be. This love of plants led to a fascination with fungi and mushrooms foraging.

As I grew older, I spent a lot of time hiking and camping in wild places, seeking edible mushrooms. Even now, I share my passion with my wife and children, as we often take family trips to the forests to identify and enjoy tasty mushrooms that we pick ourselves.

It's now been fifteen years since I began to venture into the world of foraging, and in all that time, I've gained a wealth of knowledge regarding these magnificent mushrooms. I've learned how to identify different types of mushrooms, how to cook them safely, and how to stay away from dangerous varieties. All this knowledge can be helpful to you, as well, as you begin or continue your own journey of mushroom hunting.

The World of Fungi

While many foragers turn to mushrooms as a delicious snack, they aren't only a natural food source. Mushrooms and other fungi form a foundational piece of life on earth and are the subjects of an important branch of scientific study: mycology. Mycologists, or biologists who study mushrooms and other fungi, categorize them into families, determine toxicity levels, and seek to understand how these fantastic fungi contribute to earth's ecosystems. In addition, mycology clubs and societies provide guides to foragers and aid anyone seeking to understand more of the world of fungi.

Both foraging and mycology are intertwined fields of study that rely on one another. For example, many hobbies and career mycologists are foragers themselves who spend time in the field, picking and identifying various types of mushrooms. And it's always essential for foragers to understand the fungi they are hunting.

The poet Emily Dickinson describes mushrooms as "the Elf of Plants," elusive and short-lived, adding beauty to the earth after a shower of rain and then disappearing entirely. Despite the mysterious nature of these fleeting fungi, the history of humans and mushrooms is well-recorded. It can lead to a greater understanding of how mushrooms became a culinary delight.

History of Foraging Mushrooms

Although separated by boundaries of culture and distance, cultures worldwide have always been united by common traditions and practices. These transcendent practices include creating music, using language to communicate, and foraging for wild edible foods, including mushrooms. For centuries, humans around the world have been going into forests and gathering mushrooms for food, medicine, hallucinogens, and other practical uses such as clothing dye. Some dangerous species have even possibly been used as poisons and tools for assassination (Avey, 2014)!

Archeologists speculate that humans have used mushrooms

for various purposes from as early as 10,000 BC. In the Eastern world, mushrooms were included as a popular culinary food from around 600 CE, when Japan and China began cultivating shiitake mushrooms (*Real Food Encyclopedia — Mushrooms*, 2019). The fungi might have had other uses in ancient China, as some hallucinogenic mushrooms were found and recorded in the sixteenth century by Li Shizhen, a revered herbalist in Chinese history (Li, 1977).

In the West, people tended to be hesitant to consume mushrooms. For example, mycophobia, or fear of mushrooms, dominated public consciousness due to stories of inadvertent deaths caused by poisonous fungi. This food source remained overlooked and feared until the French began including mushrooms in their cuisine. Mushrooms gained a new reputation among the public, and countries throughout Europe and the Americas began adopting this new food source (Avey, 2014).

Despite the growing acceptance, it was only in the early twentieth century that Americans began to view mushrooms as a hearty food source. Kate Sargeant, who jumped on the mushroom train in 1899 with her published cookbook *One Hundred Mushroom Receipts*, traces the changing attitudes in America: "The general opinion in this country regarding mushrooms has been, that with one or two exceptions, all forms of fungus growth are either poisonous or unwholesome.... Soon public opinion will acknowledge that the great majority of the larger funguses… is not only wholesome but highly nutritious" (Sargeant, 1899).

Sargeant gathered mushroom recipes ranging from soups to stews to purees, all gathered from English and American sources, and her prediction became the truth. Fungi began appearing more frequently as an accepted and even coveted ingredient in recipe books and cooking magazines around the century. Many twentieth-century Americans enjoyed a nice mushroom cream sauce served on toast or fragrant mushrooms baked under a glass bell (Avey, 2014)!

As a result, American mushroom hunting became a popular pastime, with the creation of foraging and mycology clubs. People even began making a living by foraging and selling local mushroom varieties. Even though nowadays mushrooms are often cultivated and sold in grocery stores, there are still large groups of people dedicated to hunting the wilds for mushrooms to eat and sell.

History of Mycology

Biology has always been concerned with the study of life on earth. Still, scientists have only recently begun to discover what makes fungi, including edible mushrooms, unique from other forms of life. For much of history, fungi were assumed to be another type of plant or vegetable. However, around the mid-1800s, when the microscope allowed a closer study of these life forms, scientists could more closely study fungi. A new field of study was born when it became apparent that fungi were quite different from either plants or animals.

Fungi studied in mycology are unique in that they have more than one nucleus that can flow from chamber to chamber within the fungus. Their cell walls are also made of unique materials, chitin, and glucans. These hungry fungi absorb nutrients and grow from decomposing plant and animal matter. Fungi also appear in a vast number of forms. In addition to the hundreds of varieties of mushrooms, mycologists study the yeast that ferments beer and the mold that produces cheese.

The field of mycology also intersects with many other fields, including agriculture, pharmaceutics, and toxicology. Fungi can be dangerous for crops, animals, and humans, so mycologists study to understand which fungi are harmful and how to cure their ill effects. Other fungi can be beneficial, providing health benefits and breaking down toxic chemicals, so mycology works to understand how best to use fungi to improve life on earth (BD Editors, 2018).

Fungi are fundamental pieces of life as we know it, and mycology does the critical work of understanding and creating an appreciation for these vast, wonderful life forms. On a practical level, mushroom hunters can use the knowledge compiled by mycologists to aid them in their foraging endeavors. The field of mycology is vital to understanding which mushrooms are safe for human consumption.

General Warning

While mushroom hunting is a fun hobby, and many mushrooms provide a valuable source of nutrition and are perfectly safe for consumption, keep in mind that not all mushrooms are safe. As with many other beings found in nature, mushrooms have natural defenses to protect against predators, including a variety of toxins. The Poison Center warns that many mushrooms that look safe may actually be a poisonous variety that can cause a host of health issues (Soloway, n.d.).

Some toxic mushrooms will give humans a mild headache, while others can cause severe liver damage or even result in death. In America, the National Poison Data System estimates about three mushroom-related deaths occur each year, with many more cases of poisoning leading to ill health effects. Most of these poisoning cases are reported by people who were confident that the mushroom they picked was edible (Brandenburg, 2018).

Amateur foragers, and even expert foragers, who go out with the intent of eating mushrooms need to be cautious and take plenty of safety measures. These measures will be explored later in the book, but for now, be aware that there are risks when you undertake mushroom foraging.

To be a forager, you need to balance the boldness to go into the unknown and the cautiousness to hold yourself back. Be extremely careful about identifying mushrooms—there are plenty of poisonous lookalikes to edible mushrooms—and be sure to thoroughly cook any mushroom you pick! As a clinical toxicologist, Rose Ann Gould Soloway (n.d.) warns, "There are old mushroom hunters, and there are bold mushroom hunters. There are no old, bold mushroom hunters!"

Knowledge is the best defense, and you've taken the first steps towards knowledge by picking up this book! But once you close this book and set off on your foraging adventure, your safety is in your own hands. Treat yourself well and pay careful attention to the information you will read in this book, the words of your local experts, and the instructions laid out by mushroom field guides.

With these warnings in mind, if you're ready to begin your foraging journey, let's get started!

KEY TAKEAWAYS:

- Humans have foraged for mushrooms for centuries, and foraging for wild edible mushrooms continues as a popular activity today.
- Mycology is the field of biology that studies fungi and are experts in the various types of fungi, including which are safe to eat and which are not.
- Take caution when foraging wild edible mushrooms; take your time identifying non-toxic species; always cook edible mushrooms.

Chapter 3:

The Art of Preparation

On my many camping and hiking foraging trips over the years, I've forgotten a plethora of small items: a good trail snack, a proper pocket knife, and even a hammer to nail down the tent stakes! These forgotten tools created funny stories later, but in the moment, all they caused was a big headache as I was trying to find, clean, and cook my foraged mushrooms.

Just like a chef needs a spoon, and a plumber needs a wrench, you need the right tools as a forager. Forgetting one piece of equipment can stall your whole trip and cause unnecessary frustration to yourself and your fellow mushroom hunters. Learn from my mistakes–make a list and double-check that you have everything you need before leaving.

For your foraging expeditions, you need to bring a variety of equipment that will help you gather, clean, and store the mushrooms that you'd like to eat. If you plan on camping, you also need to bring extra equipment to spend the night in the wild, such as a tent and sleeping bags. Although perhaps you can leave the food at home and enjoy a dinner made up of the mushrooms you collect!

So before you put on your hiking boots and step out into the wild, make sure that you're fully prepared so that you can easily find and organize your mushroom meal. When both you and your mushrooms are well-prepared, the result is a melt-in-your-mouth culinary delight!

Tools of the Trade

If I asked you to picture someone going out into the woods to gather plants, you might envision someone holding a woven basket and filling it with berries or herbs. Perhaps the most prominent tool for mushroom foraging is a bag or basket to store your mushrooms. Without a bag or basket, you'll be stuck stuffing mushrooms in your pockets or what you can carry in your hands, and you'll end up very disappointed with the amount of yummy morels and chanterelles you can gather.

Mesh Bag or a Basket

Many foragers encourage using a mesh bag or a basket with small gaps so that spores from your gathered mushrooms can fall through the cracks as you walk. In this way, you can ensure that the spores are spread, and mushrooms can continue to grow. After all, part of a forager's responsibility is to ensure that the ecology of their hunting grounds is preserved.

A large basket or mesh bag will also help preserve your mushrooms until you can get them safely home or to the cooking pan. As a chef and experienced mushroom forager, Andrei Litvinenko (2011) explains since fungi can be delicate and easily squashed, it's a good idea to give them some space and avoid overfilling a small bag. The holes in the bag can also release any clumps of dirt, making your cleaning job more manageable.

Pocket Knife

When you venture out, make sure you store a pocket knife, a small trowel, and a soft brush in your pockets or backpack. These tools are essential for safely and carefully removing the mushrooms from their environment, as well as cleaning and preparing them to be your delicious dinner!

A pocket knife can have a plethora of uses for a forager. First and foremost, a knife will help you extricate your mushrooms with minimal fuss. Rather than digging out the roots and harming the mycelium, you can simply cut the mushroom at the stem. You can also remove any growths or inedible pieces of the mushroom before stuffing it in your basket or bag. Although you can bring other knives, a foldable pocket knife will be easier to carry on a vigorous hike (Keough, 2021).

A pocket knife can also aid you in identifying some species of poisonous mushrooms. Eric Briggaine (2018), an expert forager, explains that you can cut into a Boletes mushroom and observe the coloring: any blue stains mean that the mushroom is poisonous and should be avoided. Cutting into mushrooms you pick can also help you check for the presence of worms or larvae burrowed inside the mushrooms. If you see many tunnels or white, squirmy worms, you should probably put the mushroom down and keep moving.

Garden Trowel

In addition to your pocket knife, you also need to bring a small garden trowel that can help you dig the mushrooms from the ground. Mushrooms' root systems can grow quite firmly in the soil, and some mushroom species might become too damaged if removed with a knife. In addition, there are garden trowels that can be easily folded up and stored, making them easier to carry.

Cleaning Brush

For easier mushroom cleaning and cooking, a soft-bristled brush is vital. You can use a paintbrush, a toothbrush, or a specific brush made for mushroom foragers. Use this brush to dust and dirt off the mushrooms you find before storing them in

your bag. You will not only help spread spores around the brushing site, but you will also make sure that your mushrooms are relatively clean. A brush is gentle enough to clean off the dirt without damaging the dainty fungi!

Topographic Map and GPS

In order to keep on the right path and find the perfect mushroom-hunting spots, bring along a topographic map. Some mushrooms love high elevations, while others thrive in low elevations. A topographical map that details elevation levels within your hunting grounds can show you where to head to find these mushrooms. Print one out, get one from your local foraging community, or find an app or use Google Maps since almost everyone carries smartphones these days. Just make sure that your resource doesn't require data or Wifi just in case you get out of range!

Water and Snacks

Because you will most likely be hiking and expending energy as you forage, you need to bring water and snacks. You might be tempted to munch on some mushrooms as you go, but avoid eating any uncooked mushrooms! Uncooked mushrooms won't be as nutritious. They might also contain some trace amounts of toxins that will be eliminated once cooked. Instead, bring other snacks, such as a sustaining trail mix or fruit.

Permit to Hunt

While you might want to make a spontaneous mushroom gathering trip, you need to secure a permit to hunt for mushrooms in some locations. In the Midwest, some locations require a paid permit, especially if you plan to gather a large variety of mushrooms and sell them for profit.

Yellow Vests or Bells

Depending on the season and location of your chosen foraging venture, you might need to wear yellow vests or bells to avoid hunters or bears. Suit up any accompanying friends or pets as well. Safety is the number one priority when foraging!

Is This Mushroom Safe to Eat?

While not the most obvious, a field guide is probably the most important tool you need to bring while harvesting wild, edible mushrooms. While you can prepare beforehand and be aware of what mushrooms you want to pick, mushrooms can be tricky. What you think is a delicious meadow mushroom might, in fact, be a poisonous destroying angel mushroom. The differences between these two fungi are minimal, and comparing any mushrooms you find closely against a field guide can help keep you safe.

Even better, go mushroom hunting with someone who has more experience than you. The appearance of mushrooms can change from season to season and from region to region, so finding someone who already knows the area like the back of their hand gives you a better chance of safely foraging for edible mushrooms. Plenty of foraging clubs host excursions that you can join if you're new to an area and want to learn more about which local mushrooms are safe to eat.

Above all, don't trust any mushroom too much. Instead, put it to the test. Carefully examine the mushroom and leave it alone unless you're sure it's an edible variety. If it's time for cooking and you're still not sure whether or not the mushroom you picked is an edible fungi, get together with another forager and fry up a tiny piece to try. If you don't feel any ill effects after a few days, feel free to assume that the mushroom is safe.

Cleanliness is Next to Deliciousness

Once you bring back your safe and edible mushroom haul, the next step is making sure your mushrooms are clean and ready to eat. Mushrooms grown in the wild will most likely be covered in dirt, and some might be hosts to worms or insects. While some foraging techniques such as cutting the stems or brushing them off can help minimize the cleaning you need to undertake, you need to take care to wash off your mushrooms before you toss them in the frying pan.

Sometimes, mushrooms might need to be trimmed. Trimming can consist of using a pocket knife or kitchen knife to cut away the stem, extra growths, or other undesirable parts of the mushroom. However, if you notice extensive rotting or animal bites, you should dispose of the mushroom rather than trimming around those parts.

Rinse or wipe with a damp cloth—but don't soak—the mushrooms in clean water as needed. Some mushrooms have gills or crevices that can make dirt removal especially difficult. In these cases, you may need to cut or tear the mushroom in order to clean it with water (Litvinenko, 2011) properly. However, make sure the mushroom doesn't absorb too much water, making it soggy and difficult to cook.

Some mushrooms might also contain tiny larvae or worms who love to feast on the delicious fungi. While these little bugs might gross you out, they're generally not harmful to eat; many mushrooms, including canned mushrooms, contain worms or bug parts (Levy, 2009). However, if you'd like to eat a mushroom that's been nibbled on by bugs, you can expel the worms by drying the mushrooms for two or three days. A salt bath can also be a solution for killing off these insects, although, as stated earlier, be wary of soaking the mushrooms too long and making them more difficult to cook.

Once your mushrooms are spick and span, they're ready to be stored or cooked!

Delicious, Nutritious Mushrooms

Mushrooms have become such a popular food choice not just because they are delicious as additions to meals and replacements for bread and meat, but also because they pack a lot of nutritious value in a small package. Whether they're fried, baked, steamed, or pickled, mushrooms make a delicious, savory, woodsy-tasting snack that provides nutrients and a host of health benefits for anyone looking to eat well.

Nutritionally, mushrooms contain few calories and provide fiber, protein, potassium, various vitamins, and even antioxidants. Mushrooms that are grown in the wild or are exposed to ultraviolet rays as they grow. They are a good source of Vitamin D, which will help keep your bones strong and healthy. The Vitamin B contained in these amazing fungi helps to keep your body functioning well by boosting your immune system and protecting your cells and tissues (Shubrook, 2021).

Additionally, mushrooms are renowned for boosting the immune system and helping to avoid catching minor sicknesses. For those who struggle with high blood pressure, mushrooms can reduce blood clots and lower blood pressure (Shubrook, 2021). They can also aid in weight loss when replacing beef in recipes (WebMD Editorial Contributors, 2020). Mushrooms are delicious sources of health benefits on their own or can be added to other healthy meals such as stir-frys or omelets as a supplement (Epicurious, 2021).

With all these health benefits and perhaps more that have yet to be discovered, it's no wonder that people are increasingly turning to mushrooms as a source of nutrition. Foragers and mushroom connoisseurs can rest assured that their hobby is not only fun and fulfilling but also nutritional.

Storing Your Mushrooms

Once you've gathered all the mushrooms your heart desires, you can begin cooking. After you've eaten your fill, you can easily store any leftovers in a dry place. This way, you can have a store of mushrooms to munch on for a long time to come. When storing mushrooms, it's imperative to remove as much moisture as possible from your mushrooms. Wet or soggy mushrooms are likely to breed dangerous bacteria.

If you are just getting started and don't have any drying cabinets or tools, you can simply pat dry the clean mushrooms and store them in a paper bag. While not ideal, this method will keep the mushrooms fairly fresh. Wild mushrooms go bad rather quickly when stored incorrectly, getting slimy and growing bacteria within three days.

Air drying, however, is an effective and simple way to preserve mushrooms. Put the mushrooms on a paper-covered tray and place the tray in a dry, sunlit place. If you have an empty cabinet and heat lamp, you can also place the mushrooms inside the cabinet and heat the bottom with the heat lamp. Then, as the heat rises, the mushrooms will dry out nicely. Or, dehydrators that are purposefully made to dry out food can be an easy, low-effort way to dry and preserve your mushrooms.

Freezing mushrooms is another option. While you will need to thaw these mushrooms before you're able to make any dishes with them, frozen mushrooms can last anywhere from six months to a year if stored properly. First, you need to cook the mushrooms to get rid of any harmful bacteria, and then dry them with a cloth or air-drying method. Then, place the mushrooms in a freezer bag and get out as much air as possible. If you're able to vacuum seal the bag, this can lengthen the storage time and increase the quality of your mushrooms once they're thawed. If you can't vacuum seal, you can weigh down the bag with rice or beans before sealing it to eliminate as much air as possible (Lee, 2019).

A final method of storage is to pickle or can your mushrooms. While these mushrooms won't last as long, they can be snacked on for several weeks. You can make a delicious jar of pickled mushrooms by combining cooked mushrooms with salt water, vinegar, peppercorns, and bay leaf into a jar of boiling water and vinegar and refrigerating it for one or two days. This way, you can keep your mushrooms as a crisp snack for up to a year (Bergo, 2021). Just make sure to cook any mushroom before picking it!

Mushroom Spore Prints

To help you identify a mushroom, you gather or create a piece of eye-catching art from your wonderful fungi; you can make a spore print. Typically, a mushroom's spores are invisible to the naked eye, but a spore print can help give you an idea of the type of mushroom you are dealing with.

You can compare the spore print to those found in field guides to double-check the mushroom species you have harvested. Sometimes, checking the color of a spore print is the key to distinguishing an edible mushroom from a toxic lookalike.

The spores make a spore print from a mushroom's gills or pores being pressed onto a light-colored piece of paper with the aid of water. The result is a perfectly circular imprint of a mushroom and its fanning gills. The print can be a variety of colors depending on the mushroom species.

If your mushroom has gills on the underside, you can place the mushroom gills down on your chosen medium, whether stock card paper or a simple white sheet of computer paper. To release the spores, drip a bit of water on the cap, then cover your mushroom with a bowl or cup. You need to leave your spore print alone for between 2 and 24 hours.

Meanwhile, if your mushroom has pores, you might need more water to release the spores. Instead of dripping water on the cap, you should wrap the mushroom in damp paper before setting them down to make your print. However, the rest of the process remains the same!

Spore prints are also popular as art pieces. You can frame your art or keep it in a safe place to remind you of your foraging adventures. To set your print, carefully spray it with some hairspray or artist's spray (Sheine & Rogers, n.d.). Afterward, you will have a lovely spore print that you can study and experiment with to create beautiful pieces of natural art.

KEY TAKEAWAYS:

- Take the essential tools with you into the field so that you can stay prepared.
- Never, ever trust a mushroom at first sight. Never eat a mushroom you're unsure about.
- Thoroughly clean all mushrooms with brushes and water before eating them.
- Mushrooms are powerhouses of nutrition, providing many vital vitamins and minerals.
- You can dry, freeze, pickle, or store fresh mushrooms in a well-ventilated area.
- Mushroom spore prints can be important for identifying mushrooms or creating a lovely piece of art!

Chapter 4:

Whimsical Winter Mushrooms

Wood Ear (Auricularia auricula-judae)

The unique wood ear mushroom has been used as a medicinal fungus across Europe and Asia since at least the Middle Ages and has been gaining popularity worldwide as a delicious edible mushroom!

How to Identify

The peculiar wood ear mushroom is dark brown or black in color and is shaped like a round, thin pancake, the diameter of which can be up to 7 centimeters.

It's usually attached to the tree by a thin point, fanning out to form a flat or cup-shaped mushroom. If you look closely at the edges, you should notice some wrinkling. These characteristics make it look somewhat like an earlobe, thus its nickname!

When you spot a dark, gummy-like mushroom that might be a wood ear, use your fingers to pinch and bend it. A wood ear mushroom should feel somewhat tough, not squishing between your fingers easily; however, you should still be able to fold it in half (*The Edible and Medicinal Wood Ear Mushroom: Auricularia Auricula.*, 2017).

Habitat

Look for wood ear mushrooms on dead or dying trees, logs, and stumps in forested areas. Your best bet is to search in forests with lots of beech, sycamore, and elder trees.

They grow most abundantly during the late fall and winter months, so wait to hunt for them after the weather turns cold.

How to Gather

Use your pocket knife to cut this mushroom away from the trunk. Just be careful not to cut away any pieces of dead or dying bark as well!

How to Prepare

You'll need to wash these mushrooms carefully in a bowl of water, swishing them around to make sure any dirt has been removed. Once cleaned, you can either dry or cook them right away. Once dried, you can store them for a while and simply rehydrate them when you want to use them in a recipe.

If you add them to a boiling pot of water or soup, they quickly regain their size and moisture within minutes. If you continue cooking them for about half an hour, they should achieve the perfect texture—soft enough to eat while still providing a slight crunch.

In addition to soup, thinly-cut strips of wood ear mushrooms are often used in a host of Eastern and Western cuisines, including stir-fry, stews, ramen dishes, and dumplings!

Nutritional Content/ Benefits

Wood ear mushrooms have been prized for their high nutritional value and medicinal qualities for centuries. These fantastic fungi can add potassium, calcium, copper, and vitamin B6 to your diet, meaning that they work to strengthen bones, increase heart health, and fend off blood clots. On the flip side, it is advised that anyone taking blood thinners avoid eating wood ear mushrooms (*Wood Ear Mushroom — Everything You Need to Know*, 2020).

RECIPE/REMEDY

Wood ear mushrooms are popular in East Asian cuisine, where they feature in healthy salads and as a yummy, crunchy yet slimy addition to soups and ramen (Williams, 2012). This authentic Chinese salad recipe is just one example!

Wood Ear Mushroom Chinese Salad

Ingredients:

- ¼ cup dried wood ear mushrooms
- 2 diced scallions
- ½ small onion
- 2 minced garlic cloves
- 2 de-seeded and diced red peppers

- 2 tsp vegetable oil
- 1 tsp Chinese black vinegar
- 2 tbsp soy sauce
- ½ tbsp sesame oil
- ½ tsp sugar
- ½ tsp parsley
- 1 tbsp toasted sesame seeds

Instructions:

1. Soak the dried mushrooms in cool water for 1 hour until they rehydrate. Drain.
2. Boil a pot of water on the stove. Add mushrooms and onions for 3-4 minutes. Drain and add mushrooms and onions to a new bowl of cold water.
3. In another bowl, mix together Chinese black vinegar, soy sauce, sesame oil, and sugar. Stir until the sugar dissolves.
4. Add cooking oil to a pan and heat over medium. Briefly saute garlic, scallions, and red peppers until fragrant, about 30 seconds.
5. In a large bowl, mix together the contents of the pan, the mushrooms, and the onions. Mix in the sauce.
6. Cover and refrigerate the salad for half an hour, then mix again.
7. Serve!

Adapted from (*Wood Ear Mushroom, China Sichuan Food*, n.d.).

The jelly ear mushroom has some lookalikes, but none are toxic—at most, these lookalikes are too tough to be edible. Remember to carefully identify each mushroom before you eat it.

Yellow Foot Chanterelle
(Craterellus tubaeformis)

These popular chanterelles are the perfect winter mushrooms for any forager, even a beginner. More obvious ones are bright spots in an otherwise dreary landscape, while more hidden yellow foot chanterelles are like a buried treasure you can have fun uncovering!

How to Identify

Yellow foot chanterelles are small, trumpet-shaped mushrooms with a deep dimple in the middle. They can range in color from light orange-brown to yellow. They have thin stems that are hollow inside, and their gills are usually visible. The gills are forked with blunt edges and run from the edge of the cap to the top of the stem.

If you sniff a yellow foot chanterelle, you should notice a fruity apricot smell. You can also use your knife to cut into the flesh of the cap and take note of the color—yellow foot chanterelles will be white or cream-colored inside.

Habitat

In the Midwest, you can look for yellow foot chanterelles in forests alongside patches of moss in the late fall and early winter months (Winkler, n.d.). They grow directly from the ground around beech, poplar, and oak trees, sometimes in holes or divots around the roots, so you might need to sift through the leaves to spot these bright yellow fungi!

How to Gather

Once you find a patch of yellow chanterelles, you can brush away any dirt with your hands and use your knife to cut the hollow stem close to the ground. You might be able to pinch them with your fingers as well, but the knife can give you more control, especially if you're wearing gloves in the cold weather.

How to Prepare

To keep your foraged yellow foot chanterelles around as long as possible, keep them stored in the cool fridge, as they go bad quickly if left in the open (Williams, 2011). You can choose to dry and store them, although rehydrated chanterelles have a chewy, rubbery texture.

You can pickle, roast, or fry these dried mushrooms directly for a crunchy treat. They also work well as additions to pasta sauces, winter stews, and meat pies, and many people enjoy them on top of toast!

Nutritional Content/ Benefits

These wonderful winter mushrooms can give you a host of essential vitamins and minerals, including vitamins A and C, potassium, iron, and copper. These can strengthen your immune system, reduce inflammation, and improve bone health.

Another perk of yellow foot chanterelles is their high level of vitamin D; eating a handful of them can provide you with a whole day's worth of this mood-boosting and bone-strengthening vitamin (WebMD Editorial Contributors, 2020)!

A good handful of tiny yellow foot chanterelles can add an earthy quality to a host of winter soups—you'll stay warm and get many of the nutrients you need in your day.

Yellow foot Chanterelle Winter Soup

Ingredients:

- 2 tbsp cooking oil
- 1 small chopped onion
- 2 small potatoes
- 1 minced garlic clove
- 5 cups vegetable broth
- ½ cup pasta
- 2 cups yellow foot chanterelles
- 1 tbsp cornstarch
- ½ tsp parsley
- ½ tsp salt

Instructions:

1. In a pan over medium heat, cook onions until they become translucent. Add minced garlic until it becomes fragrant, about 30 seconds.
2. Move onions and garlic to the outside of the pan. Add potatoes and cook until they begin to soften.
3. Pour in broth and let it boil, then add the pasta. Cook until the pasta is almost done, 5-6 minutes.
4. Reduce the heat and add in chanterelle mushrooms. Cover the pan and cook for 3-4 minutes.
5. Stir in the cornstarch and let the sauce thicken for a minute or two. Remove from the heat and season with parsley and salt to taste.
6. Serve and enjoy!

Adapted from (*Bergo*, n.d.).

Yellow foot chanterelles have a toxic lookalike, the particularly worrisome fungus known as the jack-o'-lantern mushroom (*Omphalotus olearius*). This orange, bioluminescent mushroom can cause intense stomach issues, ranging from pain to diarrhea and vomiting (Adamant, 2018). It's not life-threatening, but you should definitely avoid eating it!

To distinguish these mushrooms, take note of their location. Yellow foot chanterelles grow from the forest floor, while jack-o'-lanterns grow directly from trees. A close inspection of the gills and inner flesh can help you, too, as jack-o'-lanterns have straight, fragile gills and pumpkin-orange flesh all the way through.

Omphalotus olearius.

Chapter 5:

Succulent Spring Mushrooms

Bicolor Bolete (Baorangia bicolor)

Bring your camera along just in case you find one of these giants, but aim to pick only the smaller mushrooms, which have a better taste.

How to Identify

Usually, the rounded cap and thick stem are red, while the porous, spongy underside of the cap is yellow. As the mushrooms mature, the edge of the cap tends to curl up, revealing more yellow. When cut in half, the flesh inside the stem and cap is also yellow.

Like other boletes, this mushroom can grow quite large, with the cap growing up to 15 centimeters in diameter and the stem growing up to 10 centimeters in height. The stem can also grow almost as thick as the cap itself.

While the vibrant red and yellow colors make this mushroom

stand out from the crowd, their curry-like smell can also help you identify them. You can also try cutting into the flesh and looking for a very faint blue bruising, although some bicolor boletes won't change color (Kuo, 2015).

Habitat

Search for this bicolor mushroom at the end of spring, from June until October (von Frank, 2020). They appear in deciduous hardwood forests across the Midwest, especially in eastern regions from the Great Lakes to Missouri.

How to Gather

To gather these mushrooms, cut the stem with your pocket knife, leaving behind the mycelium to make sure you can come back next year to find more. It's a good idea to look for smaller mushrooms, which have a more tender taste.

When you find the perfect-sized mushroom, check the porous underside of the cap for any bug damage before putting it in your bag.

How to Prepare

Once you wash off your bicolor boletes, you can use them as a hearty addition to many dishes. Since they're generally so huge, you'll need to chop or dice them, and then you can add them to sauces and stews, saute them as a side dish, or use them as a meat substitute.

If you prefer to dry your bicolor bolete, you can grind them up and create a flavoring powder that can be used in soups and broths.

Nutritional Content/ Benefits

If you're looking for a food to strengthen your bones and immune system and keep your body running smoothly, bicolor bolete can help. This mushroom provides vitamin A, iron, zinc, and magnesium, among other essential vitamins and minerals (*Boletus Bicolor: The Two Colored Bolete Identification and Benefits*, 2019).

The savory flavor of bicolor boletes makes them the perfect choice to include in a light, springtime pâté, best eaten with toast or cut veggies as a snack!

Bicolor Bolete Pâté

Ingredients:

- 4 cups chopped bicolor bolete mushrooms
- ½ cup toasted walnuts
- ½ cup parmesan cheese
- ½ cup plain yogurt
- ¼ cup vegetable stock
- ¼ cup white wine
- 2.5 tbsp olive oil
- ½ tbsp thyme
- 2 minced garlic cloves
- ¼ tsp salt
- ⅛ tsp pepper
- 1.5 tbsp lemon juice

Instructions:

1. In the oven at 350°F, roast the walnuts for 7-9 minutes. Set them aside once they're lightly browned.
2. In a bowl, mix together the wine, vegetable stock, salt, thyme, and mushrooms.
3. Pour olive oil in a pan over medium heat, then pour in mushroom mixture and cook for 15 minutes, or until the mushrooms slightly brown. Add the garlic and cook for another 30 seconds, or until fragrant. Remove the pan from the heat and set aside.
4. Add mushroom mixture, walnuts, parmesan cheese, and yogurt to a blender, and blend for 3 minutes, or until the mixture is smooth.
5. Pour the blended pâté into a bowl, then cover and refrigerate the blended pâté until it firms up. Serve it at room temperature, and enjoy!

Adapted from (*von Frank & Durette*, 2021).

The general rule of thumb is that red mushrooms in the wild should be avoided, so be especially careful when identifying the bicolor bolete. Also, watch out for its slightly poisonous lookalike, the *Boletus sensibilis*, which will quickly turn dark blue when cut (unlike the bicolor bolete, which will barely bruise blue, if at all) (von Frank, 2020).

Boletus sensibilis.

Black Morel (Morchella angusticeps)

Morels are a staple of springtime foraging and some of the most talked-about mushrooms for beginning foragers, and black morels are one popular option that you can find in the early months of spring!

How to Identify

Black morels, like other morels, have an ovular, egg-shaped or pointed, pinecone-shaped cap that is tinged with black. The caps have a unique wrinkly texture that makes them look like a sea sponge, with rides that form ladders with large holes between the rungs.

The bottom of the cap is attached to the stem, which tends to be white when the mushroom is young and darkens when it matures. The inside of morel stems are completely hollow, an important fact to remember when identifying edible morels!

Habitat

These morels appear somewhat earlier than others, as they grow well in cooler weather, so look for black morels beginning in March.

Search for them in forests containing sycamore, ash, and cottonwood trees, especially those that have recently undergone a controlled burn—black morels grow well in alkaline soils that are rich in dead matter (Carlin, 2020).

How to Gather

Because of their hollow stems, you can easily pinch and pluck morels with only your fingertips. Leave the mycelium alone, as it can ensure that more morels will grow next season!

Check that the stem is hollow, and give the mushrooms a brush before putting them in your basket.

How to Prepare

Even if you've brushed your black morels at the site, you'll need to wash them again. The holes and ridges of morels are notorious for trapping dirt, so swirl them in a bowl of clean water to loosen the dirt. Thoroughly rinse and brush the cap of the mushroom (Watson, 2019).

Keep your fresh mushrooms in a breathable paper bag, and then place them in the fridge for a longer life. These fresh morels can be sauteed in butter for a simple treat or added to breakfast dishes, pasta meals, and hearty sauces.

If you'd like to preserve the taste of your hard-earned black morels for a long time, you can dry your morels and then turn them into an easily-stored flavoring powder for soups, steaks, and side dishes.

Nutritional Content/ Benefits

Black morels contain lots of copper, phosphorus, and vitamin D, which can protect your brain, blood cells, bones, and teeth! The best part is they pack this nutritional punch with minimal calories (*7 Incredible Morel Mushroom Nutrition Facts and Health Benefits*, n.d.)!

The earthy taste of black morels makes them popular in savory dishes and pairs well with steaks and pastas.

Black Morel Fettuccine Alfredo

Ingredients:

- ¼ cup black morels
- 2 cups warm water
- 2 cups fettuccine pasta
- ½ cup butter
- 4 minced garlic cloves
- ½ cup vegetable stock
- 2 cups heavy cream
- 1 cup parmesan
- 1 tbsp basil
- 1 tbsp oregano
- 1 tsp lemon juice
- ¼ tsp salt and pepper

Instructions:

1. If you're using dried black morels, rehydrate them in a bowl of warm water for half an hour. If fresh, simply chop them into strips.
2. Cook the fettuccine in a pot of boiling water on the stove. Once it's done, drain it and set it to the side.
3. While the pasta is cooking, heat the butter in a pan over medium heat. Cook the morel mushrooms in the butter until they begin to brown, then add the minced garlic. Cook until fragrant.
4. Pouring the vegetable stock and simmer until the stock reduces, then pour in the cream and parmesan cheese. Stir well until the sauce thickens and the parmesan melts thoroughly.
5. Season the sauce with basil, oregano, lemon juice, salt, and pepper. Stir well, then pour over the cooked pasta.
6. Serve!

Adapted from (*McGrory*, 2019).

The toxic lookalike you need to be aware of when hunting black morels is the *Gyromitra esculenta*, or the false morel. When eaten, this false morel can sometimes cause serious illness and even death.

Carefully observe both the inside and outside of any "black morel" you pick. The false morel's cap will have thicker ridges and less-distinguishable holes, making it look more like a brain than a sea sponge. On the inside, the stem of the false morel will contain some flesh, with only small hollow pockets, unlike the completely hollow black morel (*Morchella Americana*, 2019).

Checking for these two characteristics can help you avoid the toxic false morel!

Gyromitra esculenta.

Crown-Tipped Coral
(Artomyces pyxidatus)

Crown-tipped coral mushrooms might look like they belong at the bottom of the sea, but these delightful land-dwelling mushrooms are a delight for any forager.

How to Identify

These mushrooms grow in dense clusters of upright branches tipped with tiny prongs, looking similar to a coral that might grow in an undersea reef. They can range in color from white-yellow when young, tan-sandy brown when mature, and gray-brown or pink later.

Take special note of the tips of the crown-tipped coral mushroom, which will look like mi-nuscule crowns with tiny points sprouting around the edge of each frond or delicate battlements sprouting from castle towers. If all else fails, you can also do a tiny taste test—these mushrooms tend to have a bit of a peppery bite to them (*Crown-Tipped Coral*, n.d.).

Habitat

Crown-tipped corals crop up during the final part of spring and appear from June until September.

These mushrooms grow prolifically in the Midwest region, in hardwood forests containing willow, cottonwood, aspen, and maple trees (Kuo, 2007). They're saprotrophic, so look for them on mossy, fallen logs and dead or dying hardwood trees (*Crown-Tipped Coral*, n.d.).

How to Gather

You can cut away the coral mushrooms with a knife or pull them from the volva. Brush away as much dirt as you can before putting it in your bag or basket.

How to Prepare

The dense form of these mushrooms makes them somewhat difficult to clean, so you might need to chop up the mushroom first and clean it second. Rinse or submerge the chopped mushrooms, swish them around, and then use a towel or paper towel to dry and wipe away any dirt left behind.

It's best to cook these mushrooms to soften them, make them easier to eat and break down some of the chemicals that can cause mild upset stomachs in some. They can be sauteed in butter, fried in flour, added on top of salads, boiled in stews and soups, or used as a starch substitute in meals, similar to cauliflower. You can also pickle them along with other veggies for a crunchy snack!

Just don't keep them on the heat very long, as it's easy to burn or overcook these delicate mushrooms!

Nutritional Content/ Benefits

Healthful crown-tipped coral mushrooms can help keep your body running well by providing you with potassium, calcium, and magnesium. They're also a good source of protein, making them a good addition to vegetarian or vegan diets (*Coral Mushrooms Information and Facts*, 2019).

RECIPE/REMEDY

Crown-tipped coral mushrooms can lend their earthy taste to many dishes, including these delicious cracker snacks!

. . . .

Crown-Tipped Coral Poppy Crackers

. . . .

Ingredients:

- ½ cup crown-tipped clusters
- 3 tbsp parmesan
- 2 tbsp flour
- ⅛ tsp salt
- 4 tbsp olive oil
- 1 tbsp poppy seeds

Instructions:

1. Chop the mushrooms into small, bite-sized pieces and set aside. In the microwave, melt the butter.
2. In a bowl, mix together the flour, parmesan cheese, and salt. Slowly mix in the olive oil, and then the mushroom pieces. The dough should feel slightly sticky. Add a teaspoon of water at a time if the dough and mushrooms aren't holding together.
3. Shape the dough into squares or circles and place on a baking sheet covered with parchment paper.
4. Bake at 325°F for 20 minutes. Flip and then bake for another 10-20 minutes, or until golden and crispy. Using a spoon, sprinkle and press on the poppy seeds during the final 10 minutes of baking.
5. Let the crackers cool on a baking rack.
6. Serve and enjoy!

Adapted from (*Crown Tipped Coral Mushroom Croutons*, 2019).

Watch out for crown-tipped coral lookalikes such as *Ramaria formosa,* which can cause some stomach issues if eaten (*Crown-Tipped Coral*, n.d.). To distinguish the edible crown-tipped coral from other corals, you can take note of their habitat and tips. These lookalike corals might not grow directly from wood, and the tips generally won't look like delicate castle battlements.

Ramaria formosa.

Elegant Stinkhorn (Mutinus elegans)

These mushrooms are somewhat of a running joke among Midwesterners, with some people even removing them from their yards to get rid of their offensive appearance and smell. These mushrooms are perfectly viable for any forager to gather and eat!

How to Identify

Elegant stinkhorn has no cap as such but is rather a single upright stem that tapers to a blunt, pale point at the top. The color of the stalk is typically red, orange, or yellow, with a slimy green-brown coating at the top of the stem; sometimes, this slime can form a cap-like shape.

Meanwhile, the bottom of the stem is covered in pale white tissue that leads into a bulbous mycelium formation. The stem itself is completely hollow.

In addition to its incredibly unique appearance, the smell gives away the elegant stinkhorn. Their smell has been described as rotting meat or days-old dung. You might also spot some flies buzzing around these fungi (*Elegant Stinkhorn*, n.d.).

Habitat

These mushrooms grow throughout most of the year, first appearing in early spring. You can find them in gardens and yards around the Midwest, especially in mulch and compost (Singer, 2012). They also grow from rotting matter, such as dead leaves and fallen logs (*Elegant Stinkhorn*, n.d.).

How to Gather

Thankfully, you can ignore the smelly stalk of this mushroom and search for the bulbous eggs that grow below the ground (*Elegant Stinkhorn*, n.d.). Put in your nose plugs and use your trowel or gloved hands to dig around the stalk and pull out the round, white bulbs.

How to Prepare

Before doing anything else, you'll need to clean and remove the outer layer of the eggs. You can cut the end, peel away the protective sac, and wipe away the gelatin. This will leave you with a fleshy bulb of fungus that's perfectly edible.

You can easily pickle these mushrooms, saute them, or use them in a stir-fry. They're used in Chinese cuisine, although not really valued in Western recipes, so you can experiment and share what unique recipes you can create with this overlooked edible mushroom (Bergo, n.d.)!

Nutritional Content/ Benefits

Elegant stinkhorn provides some health benefits and provides vitamins and minerals like other mushrooms, although there is still a lot left to discover about this mushroom species (*Mutinus Elegans: The Elegant Stinkhorn Identification & Info*, 2021).

Despite the stinkiness of the stem, these mushrooms have a delicate earthy taste and slightly crunchy texture, pairing well with other flavors in dishes like stir-fry.

Elegant Stinkhorn Stir-Fry

Ingredients:

- 4 tsp oil
- 1 lb cubed chicken breast
- 1 cup elegant stinkhorn eggs
- 1 diced red onion
- 1 sliced bell pepper
- 2 sliced celery stalks
- 5 minced garlic cloves
- 2 tsp grated ginger
- 2 tbsp soy sauce
- 2 tbsp oyster sauce
- 2 tsp ground pepper
- 1 tbsp honey
- 1 tbsp rice vinegar
- 1 ½ tsp cornstarch

Instructions:

1. Heat 2 tbsp of oil in a pan over medium heat. Add the chicken, then sprinkle with salt and pepper. Once it's cooked through, set aside.
2. Add 2 more tbsp of oil to the pan, then add the onions. When they become translucent, add in the mushrooms, pepper, and celery. Let them cook, stirring occasionally, for 4-5 minutes.
3. In a bowl, mix together the remaining ingredients besides the ginger and garlic and set aside.
4. Once the vegetables are fragrant and softened, add the garlic and ginger and let cook for another 30 seconds, until fragrant. Stir the cooked chicken pieces into the vegetables, then pour over the sauce and mix well.
5. Cover the stir fry and let it simmer for another few minutes, until the sauce thickens.
6. Serve over rice and enjoy!

The elegant stinkhorn is a unique mushroom, but it does have some toxic lookalikes you need to watch out for; most dangerous are the mushrooms of the Amanita family, which are generally poisonous and can also grow from "eggs" like the elegant stinkhorn (Bergo, n.d.-a).

There are also several other members of the Mutinus family that look quite similar in appearance but aren't considered edible. These species have small differences; *Mutinus caninus* tends to be smaller and more blunt; *Mutinus ravenelii* has a larger head, and *Mutinus bambusinus* is much narrower and more pointed than the elegant stinkhorn.

You must carefully identify the mushroom and eggs before you eat them.

Mutinus ravenelii.

Fairy Ring (Marasmius oreades)

These mushrooms' name and appearance seem to spring straight from the pages of a storybook, as the fairy rings sometimes grow in have long been considered gateways into the fairy realm.

How to Identify

These small, brown mushrooms can grow up to six centimeters tall, with light to dark brown coloring. They usually feature a darker brown divot in the middle of the cap, with an umbrella of lighter brown cap forming a curtain around the thin whitish stem.

If you look under the cap, you can see distinct white gills that are fairly separated from one another; although with age, the edges of the cap rise up and let you get a glimpse of the gills even from a distance.

Look for the distinct white stems and dark brown divot of the fairy ring mushroom. You should also test the stem of this small, brown mushroom by bending it; while it's pliant and bendable, it's tough and not easily broken (Missouri Department of Conservation, n.d.).

Habitat

You can start hunting for fairy ring mushrooms in mid-spring, around April or May. They'll keep growing through the summer, with their season-ending around September.

They're especially tender and edible after a rainy day.

Fairy ring mushrooms grow in grassy areas, like lawns, pastures, and parks, in rings or arcs that are easily spotted in the open grass (Missouri Department of Conservation, n.d.).

How to Gather

Only gather fairy ring mushrooms from lawns that are relatively wild and free from pesticides and other harmful chemicals. If you spot some insects and weeds in your chosen harvesting field, you should be safe.

Use a pair of scissors or your pocket knife to cut the stem of the fairy mushroom since they tend to be tough. Brush off the mushroom to clean off dirt and spread some spores around the area.

Leave the parts of the mushroom below the ground alone, so they can keep growing and producing more mushrooms. You should even be able to return to the same spot later in the year to gather more!

How to Prepare

Once you get these little brown mushrooms home, you can separate the stems from the caps, as the caps are more tender and easier to eat. After that, you can dry your fairy ring mushrooms and store them in airtight container since they're easily rehydrated.

Use these mushrooms in soups and stews, or sautee them on their own or as part of a stir fry. Their nutty taste complements a wide array of ingredients and dishes. You can also add them to nutty desserts like cakes and cookies (Louise Freedman and the Mycological Society of San Francisco, n.d.)!

Nutritional Content/ Benefits

These mushrooms are low in bad fats and carbohydrates while also containing high levels of protein and fiber that boost your energy and digestive system (Collins, 2021).

RECIPE/REMEDY

These nutty mushrooms work well in desserts but also in savory meals like cheesy pastas or pizzas.

Fairy Ring Pizza

Ingredients:

- Pizza dough
- Olive oil
- Pizza sauce
- Parmesan cheese
- ¼ cup mushrooms
- ¼ cup sliced meat of choice
- ½ tsp oregano
- ½ tsp basil
- ½ tsp garlic powder
- Flour

Instructions:

1. Set out a pizza pan or stone, and sprinkle it with flour so the dough doesn't stick. Roll the dough out over the pan/stone in a circle, as thick as you desire.
2. Poke some holes in the dough with a fork, then drizzle with olive oil. Spread the pizza sauce over the dough, sprinkle with cheese, then top with meat, mushrooms, and seasonings to your taste.
3. Bake the pizza in the oven for 10-15 minutes at 450° F, or until the cheese melts and begins to bubble and brown. Let the pizza cool slightly, the slice.
4. Serve!

Adapted from (*Schmitt*, 2014).

Little brown mushrooms and mushrooms which grow in fairy rings are common, but don't assume that any brown or ring-growing mushrooms are edible fairy rings—many of them pose a risk for foragers aiming to eat their harvest. One such dangerous lookalike to the fairy ring mushroom is the *Clitocybe dealbata*, or ivory funnel mushroom, the eating of which can lead to abdominal pain, sweating, and shaking.

The ivory funnel is a white mushroom that also has a small divot in the cap and can be found in fairy rings and arcs; the difference can be found in the coloring and the gills, as ivory funnel gills run down into the stem rather than ending at the top (Missouri Department of Conservation, n.d.).

Clitocybe dealbata.

Fawn or Deer Mushroom
(Pluteus cervinus)

The fawn or deer mushroom is one of many little brown mushrooms that appear around the Midwest during springtime, although you might need a more practiced mushroom-foraging eye to pick it out.

How to Identify

Fawn or deer mushrooms are generally light brown-gray, with a splash of dark brown in the middle of the cap. While the cap usually grows flat or slightly rounded, the edge of the cap turns up with age, slowly revealing the gills.

These deep gills are white with a bit of a pink tinge, turning completely pink with age. As the biggest indicator of an edible fawn or deer mushroom is the gills, double-check that they are close-ly packed and that there is a clear gap between the gills and stem.

The stem is also white with an occasional pink tinge, either straight or curved, and sometimes broader where it meets the ground (Kuo, 2015).

Habitat

You can begin the hunt for fawn or deer mushrooms in May, during the end of spring, and you can continue looking for them all the way through October.

You can find these mushrooms in forested areas around the Midwest outside of North Dakota and the northern part of Minnesota. These mushrooms grow from dead tree matter, either from stumps or trunks that have been buried under the grass or directly on decaying stumps or logs. They prefer to grow around hardwood and conifer trees (Kuo, 2015).

How to Gather

Gather the mushroom by pinching and pulling up the stem or using your pocket knife to cut it away from where it grows.

If you plan to eat these mushrooms, look for younger mushrooms that haven't turned up their caps yet. Younger mushrooms are generally more tender and full of flavor (*Fawn Mushroom*, n.d.).

How to Prepare

After a brief rinse, you can decide whether to use fresh or dry mushrooms and rehydrate them later.

They have a light texture and flavor and can be used in similar ways to button mushrooms, dried, or cooked directly into dishes. They work well in stir-fry, soups, and broths, as their flavor is enhanced when paired with other vegetables and flavors (Bergo, n.d.-c). You can experiment and see what works best for your fawn and deer mushrooms!

Nutritional Content/Benefits

Like other mushrooms, fawn or deer mushrooms contain vitamins and minerals that can boost health. As they're not yet popular as an edible mushroom, more research is needed to find out exactly what they provide!

RECIPE/REMEDY

The light radish flavoring of this mushroom makes it the perfect ingredient for this sweet dish!

Sweet Sauteed Fawn Mushrooms

Ingredients:

- 3 tbsp salted butter
- 1 cup fawn mushrooms
- 1 large onion
- 1 minced garlic clove
- ¼ tsp pepper
- ¼ cup vegetable broth

Instructions:

1. Slice the onion and mushrooms into bite-sized pieces and set aside.
2. Melt the butter in a pan on medium heat. Add the onions, and stir occasionally. Keep cooking the onions for about 10 minutes. Adjust the heat lower if they begin to burn.
3. Add the mushrooms, mixing well. Sprinkle the pepper over the onions and mushrooms. Keep cooking for another 15-20 minutes, stirring every now and then, until the onions and mushrooms have caramelized (coated in brown, sweet substance).
4. Add the garlic and let it cook for another 30 seconds until the garlic is fragrant.
5. Deglaze the pan with the broth, mixing until the caramel is combined with the mushrooms and onions and the liquid has mostly evaporated.
6. Serve and enjoy!

Adapted from (*Caramelized Onions and Mushrooms*, 2020).

There are a plethora of little brown mushrooms such as *Galerina marginata*, also known as the funeral bell. They all can easily be confused with one another, and some of them are toxic (*Fawn Mushroom*, n.d.). You must carefully identify the fawn or deer mushroom before eating

Galerina marginata.

Half-Free Morel (Morchella punctipes)

These adorable mushrooms look like tiny versions of black morels and are a popular choice for foragers who are looking for edible springtime mushrooms!

How to Identify

These mushrooms are mostly stem, with a relatively small cap. The stems are thick, white, or off-white and completely hollow on the inside (*Half-Free Morel Mushrooms [Peckerheads]*, n.d.). You can cut the mushroom lengthwise to check this important feature.

The caps, meanwhile, look just like other morel caps: ladder-like ridges with fairly large holes in the "rungs," with a similar texture to a sea sponge. The coloring of the cap is generally dark on the ridg-es, with a golden yellow tan in the holes. The cap is attached to the stem at the tip, but the edges of the cap hang around the stem like a curtain or skirt.

Habitat

The half-free morel is another mushroom that grows in the middle to later part of the spring, from April to June.

You can search for them alongside other mushrooms on forest floors across the Midwest, specifically hardwood forests around oaks, black cherries, and other trees. Look for them around the roots of these trees, with which they form a give-and-take relationship (*Half-Free Morel*, n.d.).

How to Gather

Once you spot these well-camouflaged mushrooms on the forest floor, you can pluck the mushroom from the ground with your fingers since its stem is hollow. Leave the mycelium where it is, which will allow more mushrooms to spawn quickly in that area.

It's a good idea to cut the mushroom in half before you put it in your bag or basket to check for the telltale hollow stem. You should also give it a brush to clean the dirt and scatter some spores, which are stored in the hollow parts of the cap.

How to Prepare

The ridges and holes of these mushrooms can easily trap dirt and bugs, so give them a thorough wash before you eat them. You can submerge and swirl them around in a bowl of warm water, then dry them with a paper towel or towel.

These mushrooms must be cooked before being eaten, so don't eat them raw. You can easily saute or fry half-free morels as a yummy snack or side dish. You can also combine them with other harvested plants and veggies for a delicious stir-fry! Treat them similar to spinach, and don't cook them for very long, as they have a tendency to wilt quickly in heat.

Nutritional Content/ Benefits

Half-free morels, like other morels, contribute a lot of vitamins and minerals to your diet. They provide vitamin D and B and lots of iron, copper, and potassium. These can give you more energy and heighten your immune system, keeping you healthy enough to go out and forage for more mushrooms later (*Morel Mushroom Facts, Health Benefits and Nutritional Value*, n.d.)!

Half-free morels have a mild flavor that allows them to play well with other flavors, like in delicious stir-fry.

Half-Free Morel Stir Fry

Ingredients:

- 1 tbsp vegetable oil
- 1 cup half-free morels
- 1 small onion
- 2 minced garlic cloves
- 1 cup spinach
- 2 tbsp unsalted butter
- 1 tsp soy sauce
- 1 tsp lemon juice
- ¼ cup vegetable stock
- ¼ tbsp parsley
- ¼ tbsp oregano
- ¼ tbsp basil
- Salt and pepper

Instructions:

1. Chop the morels and onion and set aside.
2. In a bowl, mix together the melted butter, soy sauce, lemon juice, vegetable stock, and seasonings. Mix together well.
3. Heat a pan of oil over medium heat. Add the onion and cook until translucent, and then add the morels. Cook while occasionally stirring for 2-3 minutes, until the morels release their moisture and begin to brown.
4. Toss in the spinach and let it cook until it wilts, then add the garlic and let it cook for another 30 seconds, or until the garlic becomes fragrant.
5. Pour the sauce mixture over the stir-fry and let the mixture simmer for 1-2 minutes until the sauce reduces slightly.
6. Serve over rice or other starch and enjoy!

Adapted from (*López*, n.d.).

Avoid mixing up the half-free morel from its dangerous lookalike, the *Verpa bohemica*, or early morel, which can cause an upset stomach, or the *Gyromitra esculenta*, or the false morel, which can lead to more serious symptoms or even death.

These two dangerous mushrooms have stems that either contain flesh or chambers, while the stem of the edible half-free morel will be completely hollow (*Morchella americana*, 2019). Always cut open the half-free morel to check for this feature!

Verpa bohemica.

King Bolete (Boletus edulis)

There's a reason this mushroom is considered at the top of the mushroom chain and deserving of the name king bolete. These mushrooms can grow to enormous sizes and are one of the most desired edible mushrooms due to their delicious, meaty texture!

How to Identify

These large mushrooms come in light brown and reddish-brown colors and start off with rounded caps that look similar to baked bread buns. With age, the caps can flatten and turn up at the edges. This reveals the underside of the cap, which is porous and looks like a white or yellow sponge cake depending on the age of the mushroom.

The massive whitish-brown stems can grow to be as thick around as the cap at the base, al-though they become thinner towards the top, forming a triangle shape. The base sometimes bulges out and becomes rounded.

If you look closely at the top of the stem, you should be able to spot some thin white tissue that forms a net; this reticulation is one identifier of the king bolete (Tkaczyk, n.d.).

Habitat

King boletes start growing in May and mature through the summer and fall. Look for them, especially after rainy weather.

These massive mushrooms grow well in forested mountain regions across the Midwest, although they sometimes appear in lowland forests as well. You can spot them on the forest floor around the base of conifers and deciduous trees, with which they share a give-and-take relationship (Tkaczyk, n.d.).

How to Gather

Due to the large girth of the stem, you'll need your pocket knife to cut away the stem right above where it meets the ground. You should also cut into the stem and do a quick bug-check, as insects love to hide away in this handy mushroom home.

How to Prepare

Rather than washing these mushrooms with water, use a brush to clean away any excess dirt. You might also use a slightly damp paper towel or cloth, but submerging them will cause them to waterlog quickly.

Slice up this monster mushroom into bite-sized pieces, and then dry the mushroom pieces or cook them right away, as they don't have a long shelf life. However, they have a hearty, meaty texture that makes them popular as a meat replacement in many sauteed and baked dishes, and their strong nutty taste packs a punch of flavor (Bergo, 2021).

You might be tempted to throw a whole mushroom into your dish, but hold back—their taste can easily overwhelm other flavors (*King Bolete*, n.d.)! If you're hunting for boletes, your best bet might be to gather lots of friends and use your collection to make a few dishes you can share with your fellow hunters.

Nutritional Content/ Benefits

While these mushrooms might be "meaty," they're actually quite low in fat and cholesterol and high in protein, making them a healthy alternative. They also provide plenty of fiber, iron, and zinc, which can keep your digestive system and energy levels on track (*Boletus Edulis: The King Bolete Mushroom Benefits & Identification*, 2021).

RECIPE/REMEDY

Nutty king boletes are popular mushrooms in plenty of dishes, including easy spring soups! You can easily increase this recipe to accommodate all your friends and fellow forager and share your king bolete bounty.

Cream of King Bolete Soup

Ingredients:

- 2 cups sliced king bolete
- 2 celery stalks
- ½ cup boiling water
- 1 medium onion
- 1 large potato
- 1 tbsp olive oil
- 4 cups vegetable broth
- 2 cloves minced garlic
- 1 tsp salt
- ⅛ tsp chili powder
- 1 tbsp balsamic vinegar
- ½ cup cheese or cheese substitute

Instructions:

1. Dice all the vegetables and mushrooms and set aside. Boil ½ cup water on the stove, and soak the mushrooms for 5 minutes.
2. Heat the oil in a pan on the stove. Add the onions and cook for 3-4 minutes until they begin turning translucent. Add the garlic and cook for 30 seconds until fragrant.
3. Add the mushrooms to the pan, then stir in the balsamic vinegar, coating the onions and mushrooms well. Cook for another 3 minutes.
4. In a pot, heat the broth on medium-high until it begins bubbling. Add the potatoes and let them soften, then add the mushroom-onion mixture. Stir and keep cooking the soup for another 2-3 minutes.

5. Pour the soup into a blender and blend until smooth. Pour the mixture into a soup pot, and season with the salt, chili powder, and other seasonings you desire.
6. Serve with cheese or cheese substitute sprinkled on top, and enjoy!

Adapted from (*Dairy-Free Cream of Mushroom Soup*, n.d.).

WARNING

Although there are other boletes that might be mistaken for the king bolete, none are toxic. However, always carefully identify any mushroom you pick and plan to eat!

Meadow Mushroom (Agaricus campestris)

Meadow mushrooms are another springtime staple of mushroom hunting, but these lovely white mushrooms pose quite a challenge for identification.

How to Identify

These mushrooms have puffy white caps that make them look similar to white golf balls or baseballs that have gotten lost in the grass when seen from afar. From a closer vantage point, these caps are smooth with only light dimples or ridges.

The gills, meanwhile, are a pink or dark brown color. They are closely packed and straight, stopping just before the stem—you should be able to see a clear ring of empty space between the top of the stem and the ring of gills.

The stem is usually the same white color as the cap. There is a bit of variety in this mushroom species regarding the stem; they sometimes feature a barely-visible ring of flesh around the top of the stem, above which the flesh might be a pinkish hue (Kuo, 2018).

Habitat

You can begin the hunt for meadow mushrooms after the first spring rain; in fact, keep your eye out for them after any rainy day for most of the year, except winter.

Look for them in open fields and other grassy areas such as prairies, where they can easily be spotted due to their puffy white caps. You might notice them forming an arc or fairy ring on the grass (Kuo, 2018).

How to Gather

Use your fingers to pinch and pluck this mushroom from the ground. If you're having trouble, break out the knife, but make sure to leave the underground mycelium intact (*Meadow Mushroom*, n.d.). Take time to inspect the gills for the pink or brown that characterizes the edible meadow mushroom before putting it in your basket.

How to Prepare

Quickly rinse and dry these mushrooms before cooking with them. Keep fresh mushrooms in the fridge or in a room-temperature place until you're ready to use them, but make sure they're in an open container. If you try to keep them in a box or wrapped, they'll turn slimy pretty fast.

There are dozens of ways to prepare this versatile mushroom. Use sliced meadow mushrooms in stir-fry, sautee them in butter, roast them in the oven, or fry them on kebabs! Your imagination is the limit for this fresh-tasting mushroom.

Nutritional Content/ Benefits

Meadow mushrooms make for a light meal with minimal carbs and fats and plenty of vitamins and minerals. The vitamin B6, protein, potassium, and copper in these mushrooms can contribute to keeping up your energy, heart, and muscles (*Nutritional Information | Meadow Mushrooms*, n.d.).

RECIPE/REMEDY

Due to their likeness to button mushrooms, you can easily switch out any recipes that call for that mushroom variety, including this delightful mushroom and lemon rice!

Mushroom and Lemon Rice

Ingredients:

- 2 cups cooked rice
- 1.5 cups sliced meadow mushrooms
- 2 minced garlic cloves
- 3 tbsp olive oil
- 1 tsp rosemary
- ½ red onion
- 3 tbsp basil pesto
- 1 tbsp lemon juice
- ½ cup green beans
- ½ tsp basil
- ½ tsp crushed red chili flakes
- Salt and pepper to taste
- 2 tbsp parmesan cheese

Instructions:

1. Cook the rice in a rice cooker or in a pot. Steam the green beans in a colander over a covered pot of boiling water or in a rice cooker. Set aside.
2. Slice the mushrooms and onion and mince the garlic. In a pan on the stove, add 2 tbsp olive oil and add the onions, cooking them until they become translucent. Then add the mushrooms, occasionally stirring, until they begin to brown. Sprinkle with rosemary. Finally, add the garlic and cook for 30 seconds until it's fragrant. Remove from the heat.
3. In a bowl, mix together the pesto, 1 tbsp olive oil, and lemon juice until blended into a sauce.
4. Transfer the rice and green beans into a large mixing bowl, then add the contents of the pan (mushroom and onion). Pour over the sauce and mix everything well, adding the basil and crushed red chili flakes as you go.
5. Serve topped with parmesan cheese!

Adapted from (*Roast Mushroom, Pesto & Lemon Rice Salad*, n.d.).

During the spring, there's plenty of white mushrooms out in the fields of the Midwest, but not all of them are edible. While you think you're picking a delicious meadow mushroom, you could have accidentally grabbed its poisonous lookalike, the *Amanita bisporigera*, otherwise known as the destroying angel. This innocent-looking white mushroom can actually be deadly if it's eaten.

To distinguish the edible from the toxic, look at the gills and spore print. The innocent meadow mushroom has pink or dark brown gills and spores, while the deadly destroying angel has white gills and spores (*Meadow Mushroom*, n.d.).

As always, it's up to you to take the proper caution and carefully identify the meadow mushroom before eating it.

Amanita bisporigera.

Pheasant's Back (Cerioporus squamosus)

These shelf-like mushrooms grow in abundance all over forested habitats in spring, so they're a great choice for beginners.

How to Identify

Pheasant's backs have thin, flat caps that can grow horizontally from tree trunks or logs. These caps are decorated with dark brown feathery scales, which are the basis of its nickname, as they look similar to the feathers on a game bird. You might be able to find caps that are up to 70 centimeters in diameter!

The underside of the cap is porous, and these pores tend to be relatively large and visible to the naked eye. There is a bit of a stem, but it's mostly just a bit of flesh that attaches the large-cap to the wood where it grows.

Habitat

Pheasant's backs begin popping up in forests around the Midwest in April and keep growing until August. Look for them, especially after periods of rain, when they're more likely to sprout.

These mushrooms feed on dead tree matter, so look for them on dying deciduous hardwood trees or rotting logs, especially on beeches, elms, maples, and sycamores (Turi, 2012).

How to Gather

When gathering these mushrooms for food, look for smaller, darker ones, as these are much more edible than their larger, lighter counterparts. Also, check the underside—smaller, less visible pores can indicate a young and tender mushroom, while more open and visible pores mean that your mushroom might be too difficult to eat.

Once you find a good young mushroom, use your pocket knife to cut away the stem from the wood. Leave the older mushrooms as they are so that more mushrooms will grow next season!

How to Prepare

Some might say that pheasant's back mushrooms lean towards the inedible side of edibility, as mature mushrooms can be quite tough to eat. However, you can enjoy this fragrant mushroom by following some tips and tricks.

You can use a sharp kitchen knife to remove the porous underside and slice the cap into thinner layers, which allows the flesh to soften as it cooks. The thinner you can cut the mushroom, the better (Bergo, n.d.-b).

Once cut, you can cook them in a variety of ways. Sautee the mushroom pieces in butter, include them in a soup or stir fry, or even fry them up for a crunchy mushroom snack (Turi, 2012). These methods can bring out a sharp, lemony taste in the mushroom (*Pheasant Back Mushroom: Dryad's Saddle Benefits and Identification*, 2019).

Nutritional Content/ Benefits

Pheasant's back mushrooms can provide you with plenty of vitamins and minerals, just like the other mushrooms in this book. However, there's still a lack of research about the exact nutritional benefits of this edible mushroom.

Fresh-tasting young pheasant's back mushrooms can work well when fried, even if they remain a little tough.

Pheasant's Back Mushroom Tempura

Ingredients:

- ½ cup all-purpose flour
- ¾ cup cornstarch
- 1 tsp baking powder
- ½ tsp salt
- ½ tsp pepper
- ¼ cup ice water
- 1 large egg
- 1.5 cups canola oil

Instructions:

1. Slice the mushrooms into bite-sized pieces. Set aside a bowl of ¼ cup of the flour.
2. In another bowl, mix together ¼ cup flour, cornstarch, baking powder, salt, and pepper. Crack the egg in and mix for a few seconds. Pour in a bit of the ice water at a time, slowly mixing everything together.
3. Sprinkle the mushrooms with flour, and then dip them one at a time into the flour-ice water mixture.
4. Heat the oil in a pan or pot on the stove until it begins bubbling. Drop in the flour-coated mushrooms and let them fry for 2-4 minutes, turning them over halfway.
5. Scoop them onto a paper towel to let them dry.
6. Serve!

Adapted from (*Lundell*, 2020).

WARNING

Pheasant's back is a unique mushroom with no toxic lookalikes. However, don't let your guard down—as with all mushrooms, you must always take care to identify pheasant's backs before you eat them!

Quilted Green (Russula virescens)

On your springtime foraging trip through the forests of the Midwest, you might stumble upon a lovely green mushroom with a cracked pattern similar to a quilt stitched by your grandmother.

How to Identify

As its name suggests, these mushrooms' key feature is the green coloring; either the whole cap or the cracked pieces on top of the cap will have a green hue. As long as you spot this coloring and pattern, you can rest assured that you've found the edible quilted green.

Meanwhile, the edges of the cap might be a white or cream color where they run into the gills. You might notice a deep dimple in the middle of some quilted green caps.

The stem can be somewhat thick; it starts out white and fades to brown. Meanwhile, the gills have the same coloring and are tightly packed. The gills touch the stem, and the spore print is white. If you cut into the mushroom's cap or stem, the flesh will all be white.

Habitat

You can find quilted green mushrooms in Midwestern forests all throughout the spring, summer, and fall. Look for them on the forest floor at the base of hardwood or conifer trees (Kuo, n.d.).

How to Gather

The stem can grow thick enough that you might need to use your knife to cut it; if you use your fingers to pinch the stem, you might notice that it snaps like a piece of chalk. Leave the part that's underground alone to ensure that mushrooms can keep growing in this spot.

How to Prepare

After you bring home and rinse these mushrooms, you can dry them; drying can help you keep them for a longer time and can also bring out their flavor (Arcimovic, n.d.).

You can cook rehydrated or fresh mushrooms in tons of ways: saute them in butter, grill them on a kebab, add them to a stir-fry, or boil them in a soup (*Russula Virescens: The Ultimate Mushroom Guide*, n.d.). These edible mushrooms are quite useful in almost whatever mushroom-based recipe you want to make!

Nutritional Content/ Benefits

These mushrooms have antioxidant properties that can protect your health and keep your body running properly. They also can lower cholesterol and protect your heart health (*Russula Virescens: The Ultimate Mushroom Guide*, n.d.)!

RECIPE/REMEDY

These nutty-flavored mushrooms can enhance other flavors, but you can also enjoy their taste as the main flavor of a meal, like in these delicious stuffed mushrooms.

STUFFED QUILTED GREENS

Ingredients:

- 4-8 quilted green mushrooms
- 2 tbsp butter
- 2 minced garlic cloves
- ⅛ tsp salt
- ⅛ tsp black pepper
- ¼ cup parmesan cheese
- ½ cup cream cheese
- ¼ cups breadcrumbs
- 2 tbsp parsley
- 1 tbsp thyme
- ½ tsp cayenne red pepper

Instructions:

1. Separate the mushroom caps from the stems. Chop the stems and mince the garlic.
2. In a pan over medium heat, melt half of the butter. Place the mushroom caps in the pan and saute them on each side for 1-2 minutes. Set the sauteed caps upside-down on a baking sheet covered with parchment paper.
3. Melt the other half of the butter. Add the mushroom stems and cook them for 4-5 minutes. Add garlic and cook for another 30 seconds, until fragrant. Sprinkle salt and pepper. Place the contents of the pan in the fridge for 3-5 minutes.
4. In a bowl on the side, mix together the cheeses, breadcrumbs, mushrooms, and seasonings. Scoop the mixture evenly into the mushroom caps.
5. Cook the stuffed caps in the oven at 400°F for 15-20 minutes, or until the filling begins to brown.
6. Serve and enjoy!

Adapted from (*Gore*, 2020).

While most green mushrooms you spot in the woods will be edible and related to the quilted green mushroom, one mushroom that occasionally appears as green is quite deadly.

Watch out for the death cap or Amanita phalloides. Its cap can sometimes be an olive green color that, while quite different from the quilted green, can still cause some confusion. Carefully identify the coloring and identity of the mushroom before you eat it (Arcimovic, n.d.).

Amanita phalloides.

Turkey Tail (Trametes versicolor)

The turkey tail is another shelf mushroom that grows in abundance in forest habitats. Much like its fellow Midwestern shelf mushroom, the pheasant's back, turkey tail mushrooms resemble wildfowl, looking almost exactly like the fanning tail feathers of a wild turkey!

How to Identify

Turkey tail mushrooms are shelf mushrooms that grow horizontally from trees, with one side flatly attached to the tree and the other forming a half-circle fan shape. They can also form cup shapes when they grow vertically from stumps or logs.

All turkey tails have brown, gray, off-white, orange, or black and white stripes, usually with a lighter stripe bordering the rounded edge. The white underside of these mushrooms is covered in countless small pores rather than gills.

If you touch a turkey tail, it should feel somewhat leathery and rubbery and can be bent with just your fingers.

Habitat

You can start your search for turkey tails in May and return to the forest to look for them all through December.

They grow on dead or dying trees, stumps, and logs. You can

find them on the deciduous hardwood or coniferous trees which cover the Midwest (*Turkey Tail*, n.d.).

How to Gather

You'll need to cut the edge of this mushroom away from the wood where it grows, but leave some behind to ensure that these mushrooms can keep growing throughout the season. Pick more mature, large mushrooms that can provide more benefits.

How to Prepare

The texture of these incredibly beneficial mushrooms makes them tough to eat when cooked whole, so they're often dried, ground and boiled in water.

After giving them a good wash, you can dry and grind the mushrooms with a coffee grinder or pestle and mortar and use the resulting powder to make health-boosting tea or coffee (*Turkey Tail | Trametes Versicolor*, n.d.).

Nutritional Content/ Benefits

These mushrooms have long been considered medicinal in East Asian cultures, particularly Japan and China, as it works to strengthen immune systems and keep you healthy. It's a great fungi to consume in hot tea when you have a cold or flu (King, 2021).

New research also suggests that turkey tail mushrooms can work to protect the brain with its high levels of antioxidants (Alzheimer's Drug Discovery Foundation, 2021). It also provides a ton of protein, making it an excellent choice for those on a vegetarian or vegan diet.

RECIPE/REMEDY

While turkey tails aren't known for their taste, you can combine your turkey tail powder with other spices to brew a delicious latte.

Turkey Tail Latte

Ingredients:

- ½ tsp turmeric powder
- ¼ tsp grated ginger
- ¼ tsp cinnamon
- ¼ tsp nutmeg
- ¼ tsp garlic powder
- 1 tsp ground turkey tail powder

- ⅛ tsp ground pepper
- 1 tsp coconut oil
- 1 ½ cups coconut milk
- 1 tsp honey or maple syrup

Instructions:

1. Mix together all the ground dry spices.
2. Add the milk and oil in a small pot or pan on the stove. Whisk or stir in the spices. Heat the latte on medium while stirring well. Once bubbles appear, and it begins steaming.
3. Serve right away, or continue heating the latte on low for 8-10 minutes for a stronger taste.
4. Pour the heated latte into cups and add honey or maple syrup to taste.
5. Enjoy!

Adapted from (*King*, 2021).

WARNING

There are no toxic lookalikes to the turkey tail mushroom, but always be careful to identify the features of the turkey tail in the mushroom you've found. Look especially for the tellate porous gills on the underside to avoid picking its less-edible cousins, such as the harmless false turkey tail (*Stereum ostrea*) (King, 2021).

Yellow Morel (Morchella esculentoides)

Another member of the popular morel family, the yellow morel, also called the common morel or true morel is perhaps the original and most recognizable. It features a bright, honey-yellow cap that foragers of all levels drool over!

How to Identify

Yellow morels feature cylindrical caps in shades of yellow or gray, with the telltale morel pits and ridges that make them look like a honeycomb or sea sponge. There's usually a good amount of space between the ridges.

The stem is off-white or white, sometimes wrinkly, but always hollow. The bottom of the cap hugs tightly to the top of the stem, and the bottom of the stem tends to flare at the bottom (*Yellow Mo-rel [Common Morel]*, n.d.). These mushrooms can grow quite large, up to a foot tall.

Habitat

Start the hunt for yellow morels in the warm mid-spring, during April or May (*Yellow Morel [Common Morel]*, n.d.).

These mushrooms are so popular among foragers in part because of how widespread they are. You can find them mainly around dying or recently dead American elms and living white ash trees in the Midwest, anywhere these trees grow. They are particularly abundant on land that's recently experienced a controlled burn or in abandoned apple orchards (Kuo, 2012).

How to Gather

If you find these mushrooms in an apple orchard, crop field, or urban area, make sure that no pesticides or weed killers have been used recently, as these can contaminate the mushrooms. As long as there are some weeds populating and bugs buzzing around the area, you should be fine.

Pinch and tear away the stem and cap while leaving the mycelium, or use your pocket knife to cut the stem right above the ground. You can brush away as much dirt as you can on location; this will also help scatter spores that ensure the mushroom keeps growing. Once you find one, look around—odds are there are lots nearby!

How to Prepare

You'll need to clean the ridges and divots of the cap well, so it's a good idea to swish them around in a bowl of water to dislodge any dirt. Once you've cleaned the mushrooms, there are many ways you can prepare these morels.

Store them in the fridge for a few days, or dry and store them for longer in an open container or paper bag. No matter your chosen method of storage, cook these mushrooms before eating them. You can sautee them in butter, fry them up in some flour, or cook them up in a delicious entree.

Nutritional Content/ Benefits

Morels provide plenty of vitamin D, phosphorus, fiber, and copper. This means that they can help boost your energy, mood, digestive system, and even your bone strength! These benefits come with low fat and calories, which is great for certain diets (*7 Incredible Morel Mushroom Nutrition Facts and Health Benefits*, n.d.).

Morels have a distinct earthy flavor that pairs well with savory dishes like pasta, stir-fry, and even cheesy omelets.

Yellow Morel Cheesy Omelet

Ingredients:

- 6 large eggs
- 1 cup sliced yellow morels
- ¼ cup butter pieces
- ¼ cup milk
- ⅛ tsp salt
- ⅛ tsp pepper
- ⅛ tsp garlic powder
- ⅛ tsp basil
- ½ cup shredded cheddar cheese
- ¼ cup Greek yogurt
- 3 tbsp olive oil

Instructions:

1. Crack the eggs into a large bowl. Whisk in the milk and yogurt, add the butter, and stir in the seasonings.
2. Add 1 tbsp of oil to a small pan and saute the yellow morels until some of the liquid has dissipated.
3. Heat the rest of the olive oil in a pan over medium heat. Pour in the omelet mixture and wait until bubbles appear on the surface.
4. Add the mushrooms to one half of the omelet and the cheese to the other half.
5. Cover the omelet until it's cooked all the way through, then uncover and fold it in half.
6. Serve!

Adapted from (*Grier*, n.d.).

This light morel can be easily confused with its toxic twin, the false morel, or *Gyromitra esculenta*. This deceptive mushroom can cause sickness or death if eaten. However, these mushrooms can be distinguished based on small variations in its cap; false morels are more wrinkled like a brain than a sea sponge, with tightly packed ridges. It's also more darkly colored, more dark reddish-orange, or black.

Another yellow morel toxic lookalike is the *Verap bohemica* or the early morel. This mushroom looks much more similar to the yellow morel, but if you look inside, you can make the distinction. The inside of the early morel isn't completely hollow but rather filled with stringy tissue or flesh.

This hollow-stem test works on both the false morel and early morel, so it's a good idea to cut open your morels when you find them to double-check their identity based on the hollow stem (*Morchella Americana*, 2019).

Verap bohemica.

Chapter 6:

Scrumptious Summer Mushrooms

Black Staining Polypore
(Meripilus sumstinei)

They are also sometimes called rooster of the woods due to their close appearance to another clustering cup-like mushroom, hen of the woods.

How to Identify

These caps range from 2-8 inches, flat and usually white, gray, yellowish, or light brown. The edges are lighter in color and wavy. The caps themselves vary from being fan-shaped or cup-shaped, with a bit of a short, thick stem connecting it to the cluster.

Meanwhile, the cap's underside is white and full of small pores. Its spore print is also white. The caps produce an aromatic, fragrant scent that makes them seem more palatable to foragers and can lead you right to them if you follow your nose (Bergo, n.d.-a).

When this mushroom is cut or bruised, it turns black. It's not only the origin of its name, but it can also be a good test to confirm the identity of any black staining polypores you find in the woods.

Habitat

These mushrooms appear between July and September, so look for them during the hottest summer months.

They're typically found on stumps in deciduous forests or below oak trees. They grow right up against these trees and stumps in their dense clumps. These clumps are quite easy to spot, with some growing up to 32 inches wide (*Black-Staining Polypore*, n.d.).

How to Gather

You can cut away the whole clump of black staining polypores, especially since they're difficult to untangle from one another without extensive cutting and tearing. Leave some behind, so you can return to the same spot again next hunting season to gather more!

How to Prepare

These mushrooms have diverse uses in the kitchen. While they're tough to the touch, cooking the younger mushrooms can soften them up. Cut away and use the outer part of the circular cap, which is even more tender than the middle part.

Throw these mushrooms into a slow cooker or boil them for an hour or two to create delicious, earthy broths, stews, and soups. You can also dry and grind them up as a flavorful powder to add to these dishes later.

You should eat these mushrooms quickly once they're picked, or if you don't plan to use them for a while, cut up and freeze the parts of the mushrooms you plan to use.

Nutritional Content/ Benefits

These mushrooms still aren't popular edible mushrooms, mostly due to how they turn black when they're cut or touched. While black staining polypores provide vitamins and minerals like other edible mushrooms, more research needs to be done to uncover exactly what benefits they provide.

RECIPE/REMEDY

These mushrooms can be a tender, earthy addition to savory broths and soups, especially when allowed to cook for more than an hour.

Black Staining Polypore Mushroom Broth

Ingredients:

- 4 cups chopped or torn mushrooms
- 1 stalk chopped celery
- 1 small chopped carrot
- 1 bay leaf
- ½ tsp thyme
- 2 whole garlic cloves
- 5 peppercorns
- ¼ of one small onion
- 8 cups water
- ⅛ tsp salt (or more to taste)

Instructions:

1. In a pot on the stove, add all the ingredients and turn the heat on high. When the broth begins bubbling, reduce the heat and let the mixture simmer, stirring it occasionally. Let it cook for a little over an hour.
2. Transfer the hot broth to a sealable container, sifting it through a mesh sieve. Press on the mushroom chunks to release all the broth, and then discard the sifted-out mushroom and vegetable chunks. Add more salt if necessary.
3. Seal the broth and refrigerate it for use in the upcoming week!
4. Enjoy!

Adapted from (*Bergo*, n.d.-a).

WARNING

These mushrooms have no toxic lookalikes. Their non-toxic lookalikes can generally be distinguished based on black staining polypore's tendency to stain black (*Meripilus Sumstinei: The Black Staining Polypore Mushroom*, 2020).

Black Trumpet (Craterellus cornucopioides)

Black trumpets are small mushrooms that look almost like they've been charred even as they're sprouting from the ground. Their smoky flavor in dishes even matches their burnt appearance!

How to Identify

As their name suggests, these small mushrooms are shaped like trumpets or cups, with the folded caps leading down into a hollow central stem. The edges of the cap are usually wavy, with a folded-over lip. Black trumpets are dark gray to black in color (Steele, 2016).

Habitat

Black trumpets spring up in mid-July and disappear around the end of September. While they're quite easy to identify, they're difficult to find!

Look closely among the leaves and ground cover in hardwood forests, particularly beside oak and beech trees and shady creeks. You'll also have a better chance finding them on green moss, which they contrast nicely with, rather than the darker dirt of the forest floor (Midwest American Mycological Information, n.d.).

How to Gather

Once you find a patch of black trumpets, use your fingers to pinch and twist the stems. They should easily come away in your hand.

How to Prepare

Clean these mushrooms well since they tend to gather dirt in their hollow stems. Use a paper towel or your finger to clean out the inside while you rinse it well. Before cooking them, make sure to dry them well with a towel.

Cleaned mushrooms can be stored fresh in the fridge, then quickly use them in stir-frys or sautee them in butter. You can also choose to dry your mushrooms and preserve them for longer. Dried black trumpets can be ground into a flavorful powder for soups and broths or rehydrated for use in the aforementioned dishes.

Nutritional Content/ Benefits

Black trumpet mushrooms can give a boost to your brain and nervous system due to their high levels of antioxidants. They also pack plenty of vitamin B12, that works to protect your bones and boost your mood (*Black Trumpet Mushrooms*, n.d.).

These smoky mushrooms add a lot of yummy flavor to this dairy-heavy spread that makes a wonderful mushroom-based snack!

Creamy Black Trumpet Mushroom Spread

Ingredients:

- 1 tbsp butter
- 2 tbsp shallots
- ½ cup chopped black trumpet mushrooms
- 1 cup cream cheese
- ⅛ tsp salt
- ⅛ tsp pepper

Instructions:

1. Melt the butter in a pan over medium heat. Saute the chopped shallots for one minute or until they soften.
2. Then toss in the black trumpet mushrooms and cook for several minutes until all the liquid dissipates.
3. Turn the heat to low and stir in the cream cheese, salt, and pepper.
4. Once the mixture is soft and well-mixed, scoop it into a container and let it chill in the refrigerator. Leave it for at least two hours.
5. When you want to eat your spread, let it come to room temperature before serving.
6. Enjoy!

Adapted from (*Steele*, 2016).

WARNING

Black trumpet mushrooms have no toxic lookalikes, but you must always be careful to positively identify any mushroom you wish to eat.

Caesar's (Amanita caesarea)

Despite being a member of the often-deadly *Amanita* genus, the Caesar's mushroom is edible. Its name comes from its immense popularity in Italy, where it's been used in dishes since the Roman Empire!

How to Identify

These mushrooms grow from white egg-like bulbs, just like other Amanita mushrooms. When the smooth caps emerge, they are a bright red-orange color. These caps sprout from the bulb egg-shaped, then become rounded, and afterwards, grow flatter and duller with age. You should also be able to notice a brighter red bump in the middle of the cap after it spreads out.

The stem and gills are a bright yellow or off-white tan color. The stem has a distinct veil or ring of flesh that grows near the gills. The tightly-packed gills, meanwhile, don't touch the stem at all—you should notice a ring of empty space between the gills and stem.

No matter the mushroom's age, you should find the bulb or egg, also known as the volva, covering the bottom of the stem underground.

Habitat

You can find Caesar's mushrooms starting in the early weeks of summer. They last all through the fall, so you have a good amount of time to search for them (*Caesar's Mushrooms Information and Facts*, n.d.).

How to Gather

You should only gather these mushrooms once their caps are visible to avoid plucking one if it's poisonous family members.

How to Prepare

Due to its long tradition in Italian cuisine, there are plenty of tried and tested ways to incorporate Caesar's mushrooms into dishes. Bake Caesar's mushrooms in the oven after stuffing them or adding them to a casserole. You can also saute them in simple recipes and incorporate them into cheesy pasta dishes and sauces. If you don't want to cook them, you can add raw mushrooms into fresh, cheesy Italian salads!

Nutritional Content/ Benefits

This mushroom's fiber, copper, potassium, and B vitamins support your digestive system, brain, and immune system (*Caesar's Mushrooms Information and Facts*, n.d.).

You can stuff these meaty mushroom caps with delicious filling, then bake them in the oven.

Cheesy Stuffed Caesar's Caps

Ingredients:

- 12 whole Caesar's mushrooms
- 2 minced garlic cloves
- ¼ cup grated parmesan cheese
- 1 cup softened cream cheese
- 1 tsp onion flakes
- 2 tbsp chopped roasted pecans
- 1 tbsp olive oil
- ¼ tsp ground cayenne pepper
- 3 tbsp Caesar salad dressing

Instructions:

1. Separate the caps and stems of the Caesar's mushrooms. Place the caps upside-down on a baking sheet covered in parchment paper.
2. Chop the stems and garlic into fine pieces. Heat olive oil on a pan over medium heat, and saute the chopped stems until the liquid dissipates. Add the garlic for 30 seconds or until fragrant.
3. Mix the sauteed stems with the cream cheese, pecans, pepper, onion flakes, and Caesar dressing. Make sure all the ingredients are well-combined in a creamy filling.
4. Scoop the filling into the upturned caps evenly. Sprinkle the grated parmesan cheese liberally over the filled caps.
5. Bake the caps at 350°F for 20-25 minutes, or until the cheese on top browns slightly.
6. Let them cool slightly, then serve and enjoy!

Adapted from (*Savory Caesar Mushroom Caps*, n.d.).

The biggest downside to foraging for Caesar's mushrooms is definitely its numerous lookalikes in the Amanita family. It's most easily confused with Amanita muscaria, or the fly agaric mushroom, which is quite poisonous despite its fairy-tale appearance.

Amanita muscaria.

Chicken Fat Mushroom
(Suillus americanus)

Chicken fat mushrooms are a type of slimy bolete that looks like a mushroom-shaped piece of chicken covered in melting fat. This "fat," or slime, sometimes traps pine needles, as these mushrooms are found almost exclusively under eastern white pines!

How to Identify

Chicken fat mushrooms are yellow, with a rounded to flat cap. The cap tends to have some slime hanging off the edge of the cap. You can also spot some red or brown spots on the caps, especially on older mushrooms.

The smooth stem is usually dotted with red and sometimes contains a fleshy ring or veil.

These mushrooms have no gills but rather porous yellow flesh with hints of red on the underside of the cap. The spores produced by this mushroom are also reddish-brown.

This mushroom is a bolete but doesn't grow as large as some of its fellow boletes. It can grow up to 10 centimeters tall and 10 centimeters wide at the cap. When you cut or bruise this mushroom, it turns purple (Kuo, 2004).

Habitat

The best time to look for chicken fat mushrooms is just after a rain during the later summer months.

This mushroom is also known as the white pine bolete, which gives a hint to its usual growing place around eastern white pines (*Chicken Fat Mushroom | Suillus Americanus*, n.d.). Look for these trees and the accompanying chicken fat mushrooms around the Great Lakes, Appalachian Mountains, and other forested habitats around the Midwest.

How to Gather

Use your knife to cut the stem, but don't disturb the mycelium. Look for the purple bruising.

How to Prepare

Before eating this mushroom, cut away the spongy, porous under-side and the slime-covered top. You might also want to wear gloves since these mushrooms can stain your hands a reddish color.

Because not much of this mushroom is viable for eating, you might need to gather a lot of them before using them in your dish. Saute fresh mushrooms quickly since they go bad within a day. It's probably best to dry these mushrooms and store them, then rehydrate them when you're ready to include them in a stir-fry or sauteed meal (Bergo, n.d.-b).

Nutritional Content/ Benefits

These mushrooms are not extremely popular as an edible fungi, so there hasn't been much research done to analyze their nutritional content and benefits. However, like other edible mushrooms, they offer plenty of beneficial vitamins and minerals.

Chicken fat mushrooms have a stronger taste after they've been de-hydrated, so this recipe is best with dried mushrooms.

Chicken Fat Mushrooms with Ricotta Cheese

Ingredients:

- ¼ cup chicken fat bolete mushrooms
- 8 cups whole milk

- 2 tsp salt (or more)
- 3 tbsp lemon juice

Instructions:

1. Clean the chicken fat mushrooms well. Place them in the oven and roast them for 15 minutes at 350F. Then place them in a bowl of milk, cover the bowl, and let the mushrooms rehydrate for an hour in the refrigerator.
2. Pour the milk through a colander and set aside the whole mushrooms. Blend the milk well in a blender.
3. Add milk to a large pan, and heat it over medium heat. Sprinkle in the salt. Stir the milk occasionally.
4. Continue heating the milk until you see a good amount of steam and bubbles, as well as a light film on the surface.
5. At this point, lower the heat. Stir in the lemon juice. Stir vigorously until you see the clumps of white curds forming and the milk turning yellow.
6. Take the pot off the heat and let it stand for 20 minutes, then scoop the curds into a cheesecloth-lined colander. Squeeze out and let the curds drip dry in the cheesecloth for several minutes.
7. Store the cheese in the refrigerator or freezer and use it on many delicious dishes.
8. Enjoy!

Adapted from (*Bergo*, n.d.-b).

WARNING

This mushroom has no toxic lookalikes, but you must always confirm the identity of any mushroom you plan to eat.

Granulated Bolete (Suillus granulatus)

Granulated bolete is also called the weeping bolete due to its tendency to secrete milky fluid from its stem.

How to Identify

This bolete mushroom has similar characteristics to other boletes: its cap is rounded and brown, appearing almost like a potato when looked at from above. Rather than gills, the granulated bolete has a yellow, spongy, porous underside. The edges of the cap can turn up to reveal the gills as the mushroom ages.

The stem is thick and white, with lots of pores that leak a white, milky fluid when the mushroom is young—this fluid can also leak from the pores beneath the cap.

The flesh inside the stem and cap is an extremely pale yellow.

The cap can grow up to 10 centimeters across, and the stem can reach heights of around 8 centimeters at its biggest (*Suillus Granulatus*, n.d.).

Habitat

Granulated boletes appear all throughout the summer and autumn months.

As with other Suillus mushrooms, the granulated bolete is associated with pine trees—in this case, with Monterey pines, a tree exclusive to the West coast. So in the Midwest, you can search for them around any pines or coniferous trees where other Suillus mushrooms might grow (Mycological Society of San Francisco, n.d.).

How to Gather

When hunting these mushrooms for culinary purposes, look for smaller and younger mushrooms that are more tender and less slimy. Cut the thick bolete stem above the ground with your knife. Check for any insects inside the stem before putting it in your basket.

How to Prepare

Before eating this mushroom, you must cut away the porous underside and the slimy top, keeping only the white middle flesh.

You can easily fry to saute these mushrooms with simple ingredients. Many forager cooks opt to pickle this mushroom, saving it for a crunchy snack.

Nutritional Content/ Benefits

No research has been done on the nutritional benefits of this mushroom, but they certainly offer important vitamins and minerals that boost your health.

RECIPE/REMEDY

These boletes aren't as popular as some of their kin, with a milder taste than the king bolete, but this mushroom still has a spicy kick that makes it a delicious addition to sauteed dishes and stir-fry (*Granulated Bolete Mushrooms*, 2018).

Sauteed Granulated Bolete

Ingredients:

- ½ cups parsley leaves
- 3 minced garlic cloves
- 5 tbsp olive oil
- ½ tsp salt
- 2 lb. granulated bolete
- 1 tbsp lemon juice
- ⅛ tsp crushed red chili flakes
- ⅛ tsp salt
- ⅛ tsp pepper

Instructions:

1. Chop the parsley leaves well and mince the garlic clove.
2. In a bowl, mix together the minced garlic, 4 tbsp olive oil, and salt. Add the mushrooms to the bowl and stir to coat the mushrooms with the garlic oil mixture.
3. In a pan on medium heat, heat the rest of the olive oil. Saute the mushrooms in the oil until they begin to brown.
4. Pour the mushrooms into a bowl, then mix with the chopped parsley and lemon juice. Add the seasonings and mix once more.
5. Serve and enjoy!

WARNING

This mushroom has no toxic lookalikes, but you must be careful when foraging for any mushrooms. Double-check the identity of any mushroom you plan to eat.

Hedgehog Mushroom
(Hydnum repandum)

The popular foraging mushroom, the hedgehog mushroom, is named because it features small spikes hanging underneath the cap. These little spikes look strikingly like the little spines on the back of a hedgehog.

How to Identify

The cap of the hedgehog mushrooms features a deep pimple that looks like a belly button. The color of the cap is usually white or tan brown, with some hints of orange. The edge of the cap tends to wave and turn up, revealing the unique spiky teeth on the underside. The stem is white and somewhat thick.

Habitat

In the Midwest, you can find hedgehog mushrooms at the start of summer and up to the start of fall. These coveted mushrooms are, unfortunately, quite tricky to find in the wild, as they might be found anywhere trees grow. Look for them in forests all over the Midwest, where they grow on their own or in large groups (*Hedgehog Mushroom*, n.d.).

How to Gather

Use your pocket knife to cut away the stems and caps. Trim away any excessively dirty pieces before putting them in your bag or basket (Sayner, 2021).

How to Prepare

Trim away the spines once you get these mushrooms home, and then clean the undersides. Some chefs like to keep the spines intact, in which case you need to wash them carefully by swirling them through the water and using a brush on them, as dirt can easily get trapped there.

Once you've prepared the hedgehog mushroom, you can cook it in a variety of ways. Use them in Mediterranean dishes, nutty pies, stuffings, or sweet sauteed meals and pasta. They also work well in cheesy egg tarts and omelets (*Foraging in Minnesota: Hedgehog Mushrooms – Never A Goose Chase*, 2020)!

Nutritional Content/ Benefits

Hedgehog mushrooms are high in both iron and protein, making them a nutritional substitute for meat. Their vitamins and minerals work to reduce stress, increase energy, reduce blood clotting, and strengthen your bones. These mushrooms might be cute, but the nutritional value they provide is powerful (Sayner, 2021)!

RECIPE/REMEDY

Sweet and nutty hedgehog mushrooms work well as a main ingredient in pasta sauces, which perfectly showcase mushrooms as edible wonders.

Hedgehog Penne

Ingredients:

- 1 tbsp olive oil
- 1 tsp butter
- ¾ thinly sliced leek
- 2 tsp minced sage
- 6 cups chopped hedgehog mushrooms
- ¾ cup half-and-half
- 1 tsp salt
- ½ tsp pepper
- 1 cup penne

Instructions:

1. Set a water-filled pan on the stove. Add a dash of olive oil, pour in the penne, and boil the water. Let the pasta cook until it's tender and ready.
2. In a pan over medium heat, heat oil and butter. Add the sliced leeks, sage, and mushroom and saute them until the mushrooms are tender and begin to brown.
3. Pour in the half-and-half and sprinkle in the salt and pepper. Mix well. When the liquid begins to bubble, lower the heat and let it simmer until the mixture thickens slightly.
4. After you drain the pasta, combine it with the mushroom sauce.
5. Serve and enjoy!

Adapted from
(*Hedgehog Mushrooms and Bacon Pasta – Nordic Forest Foods*, 2020).

WARNING

Hedgehog mushrooms have no toxic lookalikes, especially with their hanging spikes and deep dimples. However, always carefully confirm the identity of whatever mushroom you pick and plan to eat.

Horse Mushroom (Agaricus arvensis)

Another prized, edible white field mushroom is the horse mushroom, so named for its tendency to grow in pastures and fields alongside horses and other livestock.

How to Identify

Horse mushrooms have rounded white or light yellow caps that grow up to 13 centimeters across. The caps tend to flatten as the mushroom matures. The edge of the cap normally has a bit of skirt-like flesh that hangs just over the edge.

The closely-packed gills are white-gray or pink and darken to brown with age. There should be a ring of empty space between the gills and the stem. Meanwhile, the stem can be quite thick and white.

There is also a white veil that starts out close to the gills and descends down the stem with time. You can spot a cogwheel pattern on the bottom of this characteristic veil (Kuo, 2017).

When this mushroom is cut or bruised, it turns yellow—except the stem, which stays white. It also smells similar to almonds or licorice, sweet and appetizing.

Habitat

Horse mushrooms crop up in the summertime and last through the fall. Search for them throughout the Midwest in grassy fields, prairies, and suburban or urban lawns. They're usually quite easy to spot due to their white color and large size, as their average diameter is somewhere between 10 and 25 centimeters (Kuo, 2004).

How to Gather

Use your knife to cut the stem of whatever mushrooms you choose to gather.

Since these mushrooms are in decline in wild habitats, use some conservation techniques such as brushing some pores into the area, taking only a portion of the mushrooms you find, and leaving the underground root system untouched as you gather these mushrooms. Do your part to preserve these wonderful mushrooms for future foragers, including yourself!

How to Prepare

Clean these mushrooms well before eating them, especially the gills. These mushrooms will stay edible for at least a week if you store them in an open paper bag in the fridge. You can also dry them and preserve them longer or pickle them for a crispy future snack (*Horse Mushrooms Information and Facts*, n.d.).

These mushrooms are easy to prepare in many ways, such as sauteing, grilling, or boiling, which is part of their popularity. You can incorporate them into pasta sauces, savory soups, delicious omelets, and as a side to meaty entrees.

Nutritional Content/ Benefits

The vitamin D in horse mushrooms can help boost your mood and give you energy, along with providing nutrients for your face and skin. This fantastic fungus also contains essential vitamins and minerals like iron, zinc, copper, and potassium, all of which contribute towards energy, healthy blood pressure, and a strong immune system (*Horse Mushrooms Information and Facts*, n.d.).

The sweet and crispy taste of horse mushrooms are great for broths and creamy soups, especially since their taste can then be incorporated into other meals in the future!

Cream of Horse Mushroom Soup

Ingredients:

- 6 cups fresh horse mushrooms
- 3 cups heavy cream
- 2 cups vegetable stock
- 1 large potato
- 1 large onion
- 2 minced garlic cloves
- 2 tsp thyme
- 2 tbsp unsalted butter
- 2 tbsp olive oil
- 1 tsp salt
- 1 tsp pepper
- 1 tsp mustard powder
- 1 tbsp sherry vinegar

Instructions:

1. Chop the onions and mince the garlic. In a pot, heat the olive oil and butter. Saute the onions until they just begin caramelizing. Toss in the mushrooms and seasonings and cook until the mushrooms soften. Then add the garlic and cook for another 30 seconds, or until the garlic turns fragrant.
2. Pour in the vegetable stock. Once it heats and bubbles, add the potatoes and continue cooking on medium-high until they're mostly soft. Pour in the sherry vinegar and stir for a minute or two.
3. Pour the hot soup into a blender and blend it until the soup is smooth. Strain it through a mesh strainer and into a storage container to remove any chunks.
4. Store in the refrigerator for a week or so, or use immediately!

The yellow stainer, or *Agaricus xanthodermus*, is a toxic lookalike of the horse mushroom (*Horse Mushrooms Information and Facts*, n.d.). If you find a mushroom that stains yellow when cut, cut the stem as well. If the stem's flesh remains white, odds are good that you've actually found the edible horse mushroom.

Agaricus xanthodermus.

Old Man of the Woods
(Strobilomyces strobilaceus)

With its curved stalk and shaggy grayish cap, the man of the woods mushroom certainly resembles its namesake!

How to Identify

This mushroom's most noticeable feature is its shaggy, scaly cap. The rounded cap features a mixture of grayish colors, from an almost-white to black. Usually, the cap is light gray, and the shaggy scales are dark. It's a bit smaller than some boletes, with its cap growing to about 15 centimeters in diameter (Kuo, 2013).

The shaggy nature of the mushrooms extends to the edges of the cap, where you can sometimes spot a bit of a ragged veil hanging around the edge like a curtain. Bits of tissue also form rings around the stem, either one or two.

The old man's gray-black stem can sometimes curve; like other boletes, it's sometimes larger at the bottom. Also, like boletes, the underside of the cap is porous and gray rather than the gills.

Habitat

Forage for old man (men?) of the woods throughout the summer and fall, from July to October (*The Old Man of the Woods Mushroom Facts*, 2021). You can search along the forest floor in hardwood forests across the Midwest, especially around oak and pine trees (*Old Man Of The Woods*, n.d.). Keep your eye out for them on foraging trips through the lower parts of the Appalachians and Ozarks, where these mushrooms might be more likely to grow.

How to Gather

It can be tough to gather a lot of these mushrooms since they tend to grow by themselves. Be patient when looking for them. When you find a young one with a very rounded cap, use your knife to cut the stalk (*Old Man Of The Woods | Strobilomyces Floccopus*, n.d.).

How to Prepare

Cook this mushroom well before eating it. Don't be put off by how the flesh tends to darken quickly after cutting; it's still good. Cut away the porous underside and, if you prefer, the shaggy cap, and use the flesh from the inner cap and stem to create your culinary delights. Use these mushrooms as meat substitutes in casseroles and other hearty dishes, where they can add a dense earthiness that's a delight to eat.

Nutritional Content/ Benefits

The general unpopularity of the old man of the woods as a culinary mushroom means that there's no information available about its exact benefits. However, like all edible mushrooms, you can gain lots of vital minerals and vitamins by chowing down on this overlooked treat.

RECIPE/REMEDY

While grilled cheese is delicious on its own, adding an earthy mushroom instead of ham or cheese can make for a delightful vegetarian or vegan eating experience!

Mushroom and Garlic Grilled Cheese

Ingredients:

- 1 tbsp olive oil
- ½ lb sliced old man of the woods mushrooms
- 2 tbsp butter
- 2 minced garlic cloves
- ½ tsp crushed red chili flakes
- 1 tsp oregano
- 1 tsp lemon juice
- ⅛ tsp salt
- ⅛ tsp pepper
- 8 slices sourdough bread
- 1 cup grated mozzarella cheese
- 1 cup grated cheddar cheese
- 2 tbsp butter

Instructions:

1. In a pan, add oil and butter and heat on medium. Saute the mushrooms until the liquid dissipates and they begin to brown. Stir in the garlic and seasonings, and cook until the garlic becomes fragrant about 30 seconds. Take off the heat.
2. Lay out the bread in pairs, cover one side with the cheese, then the mushroom mixture. Add the second piece of bread on top.
3. In a separate pan, melt the butter and toast the sandwiches on both sides until the cheese melts and the bread browns nicely.
4. Serve and enjoy!

Adapted from (*Ryder*, 2020).

WARNING

This elderly mushroom has no toxic lookalikes that can easily be confused with it. Keep an eye out for its shaggy appearance and tendency to turn red and black when cut, which can be a good test if you're still unsure of your foraged mushroom's identity.

Orange Peel Mushroom (Aleuria aurantia)

On your foraging trip or simple jaunt through the woods, if you find an orange peel that's been discarded by the side of the trail, take a closer look. You might have just found a unique mushroom called the orange peel mushroom! This bright orange fungus is eye-catching and fairly abundant, so it's a great choice for amateur hunters.

How to Identify

These interesting mushrooms appear as thin, bright orange discs or cups that sprout from the earth. They're usually between 3-10 centimeters across. The caps often develop a wavy edge that turns up to reveal the lighter orange underside. This pale, spore-covered underside is also hairy to the touch when young and relatively hairless when old (Kuo, 2020).

Habitat

These mushrooms like warmth, so they start sprouting in the early summer and last into the fall (Nelson, n.d.).

Thankfully for beginners and more casual foragers, orange peel mushrooms like to grow in places where humans frequently move about. Search for them in the clay soil alongside hiking trails, park trails, and roadsides. Even closer to home, they might crop up in your garden or yard, especially in areas covered by wood chips (Kuo, 2020).

How to Gather

Make sure to avoid picking any mushrooms that have grown by the roadside or in areas covered in pesticides or weed killers; when you find them in parks or gardens, the presence of bugs or weeds nearby means that the mushrooms should be safe to eat.

Cut the base of the disc or cup where it sprouts from the ground, and quickly brush away any dirt that might have fallen into the deep divot of the cup-shaped mushrooms.

How to Prepare

These mushrooms don't require much preparation to cook besides a quick rinse. Since orange peel mushrooms are rather brittle and don't have a strong taste, it's best to cook them for quite a while to soften them up a bit.

Most often, this mushroom is used as a salad topping, adding a splash of color to the meal (*Aleuria Aurantia, Orange Peel Fungus*, n.d.). However, you can also add it to pasta meals or stir-fry that already have many flavors, which can serve as an interesting, healthy supplement!

Nutritional Content/ Benefits

While completely edible, this mushroom hasn't gained popularity yet in the kitchen. More research needs to be done on the specific benefits of the orange peel mushroom, but rest assured that this fungus provides vitamins and minerals that will contribute to your body's wellbeing.

Orange peel mushrooms lend their vibrant orange color and mild taste to whatever dish they're in, such as this flavorful pasta.

Shrimp and Mushroom Pasta

Ingredients:

- 1 cup ravioli
- 1 tbsp olive oil
- 1.5 cups shrimp meat
- 1 cup sliced orange peel mushrooms
- 1 minced garlic clove
- 1 cup alfredo sauce
- ¾ tsp grated orange peel
- ⅛ tsp pepper
- ⅛ tsp salt

Instructions:

1. Boil the ravioli in a pan of water on the stove until it softens.
2. Meanwhile, add the oil to a pan on the stove and heat the olive oil on medium heat. Add the shrimp meat and cook it until the shrimps turn slightly pink.
3. Add the orange peel mushrooms and cook them alongside the shrimp until the mushrooms are soft and the shrimps are thoroughly pink. Add the garlic and cook for another 30 seconds until fragrant.
4. Pour in the alfredo sauce and cook for 1 minute, until the sauce begins to bubble slightly.
5. Grate the orange peel into the sauce along with salt and pepper.
6. Serve!

WARNING

With its bright orange color and cup shape, the orange peel mushroom has no toxic lookalikes. Still, always confirm the identity of any mushroom before eating it.

Oyster Mushroom
(Pleuroyus ostreatus)

Continuing the mycological tradition of naming mushrooms after the foods or animals they resemble, the oyster mushroom gets its name because it looks just like the meat inside an oyster. All it's missing is the pearl!

How to Identify

Oyster mushrooms are shelf-shaped mushrooms that grow up tree trunks or vertically from logs and stumps. The caps are circular, flat, and white, sometimes with wavy edges. There are clear gills on the underside. These gills run down into the stem of the mushroom, which is attached to the tree. There is usually a divot in the cap where the stem begins.

Habitat

Start hunting for oyster mushrooms in late summer, during September. You can find these mushrooms growing from both dead and living trees, logs, and stumps. Look for them in forests with lots of hardwood or conifer trees (Kuo, 2017). Search for them, especially in shady areas where they love to grow (Kirkpatrick, 2021).

How to Gather

Gather the mushrooms within your reach by using your knife to cut them away from the tree or use your finger to snap away thinner stems (Kirkpatrick, 2021). Try to leave part of the stem attached to the tree.

How to Prepare

You can keep fresh mushrooms in your fridge for about a week, as long as you store them in a breathable paper bag. Otherwise, you can dry and store them for longer.

Clean the mushrooms in running water, especially the gills, and pat away any excess moisture. Also, trim away any dirty places or pieces of rotting bark that you might have carried away with your mushroom.

Because of their coveted sweet, woody taste, these mushrooms are the star ingredient in stir-fry, casseroles, and simple sauteed meals. You don't have to add much to these mushrooms to make them burst with flavor.

Nutritional Content/ Benefits

In addition to brain-protecting antioxidants, oyster mushrooms also contain vitamins and minerals that boost the digestive system and energy levels, such as magnesium, potassium, and fiber. Oyster mushrooms are also low-calorie foods, which are great for certain diets (Kirkpatrick, 2021).

RECIPE/REMEDY

These prized edible mushrooms only need a few simple ingredients to make a delicious meal.

Garlic Butter Oyster Mushroom Pasta

Ingredients:

- 1 cup pasta
- 1.5 lb sliced oyster mushrooms
- 2 tsp olive oil
- 1 tsp soy sauce
- 1 tbsp butter
- 1 minced garlic clove
- ⅛ tsp thyme
- ⅛ tsp pepper
- ⅛ tsp crushed red chili flakes

Instructions:

1. Boil the pasta in a pot of water until it's tender.
2. Heat the oil in a pan on the stove over medium heat. Add the sliced mushrooms to the oil and cook them until they're browned on both sides.
3. Drop in the butter and let it melt slightly, then add the garlic to the middle of the pan and let it cook for 30 seconds, until fragrant.
4. Sprinkle the seasonings over the mushrooms and mix the contents of the pan well.
5. Once the mushrooms are soft and everything is well-coated, remove from the heat. Combine the mushrooms with the drained pasta.
6. Serve and enjoy!

Adapted from (*Nilsson*, 2021).

Watch out for a ghoulish lookalike to the oyster mushroom: the jack-o'-lantern (*Omphalotus olivascens*). Eating this mushroom can cause stomach issues such as nausea, vomiting, upset stomach, and bad cramps.

While these mushrooms have a similar appearance, look closely at the colors to differentiate them. Oyster mushrooms are always white, but jack-o'-lanterns are bright orange, almost like a pumpkin (Carlin, 2020).

Omphalotus olearius.

Purple-Spored Puffball
(Calvatia cyathiformis)

In the summer, you can find these white puffballs that are almost indistinguishable from their cousins, the giant puffballs. But if you return in the winter, you can see how these puffballs get their names, as they develop a lovely purple color—that is, before they burst in a shower of purple spores!

How to Identify

This puffy mushroom has the same shape as other puffballs, fluffy and rounded; as it grows, it forms a shape more like an upside-down pear. There is a stem, which only becomes clear with age.

The purple-spored puffball starts out completely white but soon develops a cracked brown surface, making it look like toast-ed bread or a potato. When it matures, even more, the mushroom undergoes another transformation and turns somewhat purple.

Eventually, this mushroom will burst and spray out purple spores, leaving a deflated mushroom behind. They can grow somewhat large, like other puffballs, with a diameter that can reach 20 centimeters (Folden, n.d.).

Habitat

Seek out these mushrooms when they're most edible in the summer, although you can also find them in the fall and winter. Look for this mushroom all around the Midwest, usually in arcs and fairy rings across lawns, scruffy turfs, or forest floors (Folden, n.d.).

How to Gather

Cut the mushroom at the stem, making sure not to disturb anything below the ground.

Pick the small white mushrooms before they develop the cracked skin. Cut the mushroom open to double-check that the inside is only made up of white flesh and that there are no bugs hiding inside.

How to Prepare

This meaty mushroom is easy to use in the kitchen and easy to prepare. Simply wipe or cut away any dirt and any tough parts that have developed on the outer skin. Don't wash it, as it can quickly become waterlogged (Boone, 2019).

Then you can chop up the mushroom into smaller pieces and use it in almost any dish you can imagine, from bakes to stir-fry and casseroles.

Nutritional Content/ Benefits

Puffball mushrooms are great for providing you with minerals that keep your body running well, including manganese and phosphorus (*Puffball Mushrooms Information and Facts*, n.d.).

These mushrooms add a lot of meat but not much flavor. You can cook the purple-spored puffball in dishes that have their own strong flavors, like curries, chilis, and complex soups.

Stir-Fried Spicy Thai Puffball

Ingredients:

- 1 cup puffball mushrooms
- 1 cup water chestnuts
- 1 tsp crushed red chili flakes
- 1 tbsp red curry paste
- ½ cup water
- 1 tbsp lime juice
- 1 tbsp olive oil
- 1 tsp fish sauce
- ½ tsp honey

Instructions:

1. Heat the oil in a pan over medium heat and add the water chestnuts and red chili flakes. Heat them for 2 minutes, then add the puffball mushrooms and cook everything for another minute.
2. Add red curry paste and saute for 1 minute, then pour in the water. Stir everything well.
3. Pour in the lime juice, olive oil, fish sauce, and honey, and cook until the mushrooms are soft and tender.
4. Serve and enjoy!

Adapted from (*Stir Fried Spicy Thai Puffball Mushroom With Pork*, 2016).

As with other puffballs, you might confuse the early-stage purple-spored puffball with the deadly *Amanita* mushrooms in their early stages. Always cut your puffballs in half to confirm that it doesn't contain any hint of a stem or cap. If all you see is white, solid flesh, you're good to go!

Amanita virosa.

Rooting Shank
(Hymenopellis furfuracea)

At their tallest, gigantic rooting shank, mushrooms tower over the other fungi, grasses, stumps, rocks, and ground-cover plants that grow in its vicinity.

How to Identify

Rooting shanks come in various sizes, with caps anywhere from 1.5 to 12 centimeters across and stems anywhere from 4 to 16 centimeters in height. No matter the size, the tall, slender stem will always be much longer than the cap is wide.

The gray-brown or yellow-brown cap is usually rounded or bell-shaped when young and flat as it ages. The edge of the cap is sometimes wavy and sometimes turns up to reveal the gills underneath. These gills aren't very closely packed and have varying lengths, with the longest ones running slightly down into the stem.

The long stem is usually brown towards the earth and white towards the top, often with a scaly pattern in older mushrooms. If you pulled up this mushroom, you would find a lengthy, tapered root that's sometimes as long as the above-ground stem (Kuo, 2014)!

Habitat

Rooting shank season extends from May to October, encompassing the whole of summer, so you have plenty of time to search for them in the forests or fields (Emberger, 2008).

These mushrooms appear to sprout directly from the grassy fields, lawns, gardens, or forest floors in which they're often found. The truth is that rooting shanks grow around rotting hardwood trees, so when you find one, you should be able to assume the presence of buried wood or a stump nearby (Kuo, 2014).

How to Gather

Search for the smaller rooting shanks, which are much more practical for foragers to harvest than their towering counterparts. To harvest, use your finger to pinch and twist the stem, or use your knife to cut the stem where it meets the ground. Leave the long mycelium where it is, as it's not very useful.

How to Prepare

Carefully wash out the gills, which can house dirt and small bugs. You can chop up both the stem and cap and experiment with them as you please, frying them in a simple flour mixture like other fried veggies or sauteing them in butter for a simple snack.

Nutritional Content/ Benefits

More research needs to be done on the health benefits of this particular mushroom, but they offer antioxidants and other vitamins and minerals just like other mushrooms do!

This mushroom has a mild smell and taste, but it works well in soups and fried dishes!

Rooting Shank Mushroom Rice

Ingredients:

- 2 cups sliced rooting shank mushrooms
- 2 cloves minced garlic
- 3 tbsp butter
- ¼ tsp thyme
- ¼ tsp pepper
- ⅛ tsp salt
- 1 cup uncooked rice
- 1.5 cups vegetable broth
- 1 tbsp chopped parsley

Instructions:

1. Melt the butter in a pan over medium heat. Add the mushrooms and cook until they soften, then season the mushrooms with thyme, pepper, and salt. Push to the outside and add the garlic. Cook until the garlic is fragrant, about 30 seconds.
2. Pour the mushrooms into the bottom of a rice cooker. Pour in the uncooked rice and broth on top of the mushrooms. Turn on the cooker and leave the rice to cook.
3. When the rice is finished cooking, uncover and mix up the mushrooms and rice well.
4. Serve and enjoy!

Adapted from (*Mushroom Rice*, 2021).

WARNING

The tall and graceful rooting shank has no toxic lookalikes, but you must always be cautious when picking mushrooms you plan to use in the kitchen!

Shaggy Mane (Coprinus comatus)

If you ever run out of ink to write or paint with, just find one of these shaggy mane mushrooms and wait a day or two for it to melt into a puddle of black goo. This goo can be used for writing and dyeing or as food coloring in baking!

How to Identify

The cap of the shaggy mane mushroom is, well, shaggy. It's almost completely white and covered in feathery brown- or black-tipped scales. The caps begin life deeply rounded and almost egg-shaped, hugging close to the stem, almost like a closed umbrella. Over time the umbrella opens up, and the cap flattens, sometimes revealing the gills and thin, white stem underneath.

These gills also change over time, starting out pink but growing black and gooey. This goo sometimes drips from the edges of the cap in long, inky drops. At the point that the goo starts dripping, the mushroom is close to decomposing.

Habitat

Hunt for the unique shaggy mane during September and October. The season is short because these mushrooms have fairly short lives, so get out there fast!

You don't have to travel very far to find this mushroom, as they grow in urban locations and places that are disturbed by humans. Look for them in gardens and landscaped areas that are covered in wood chips, by roads and parking lots, along park trails, and on lawns (Johnson, n.d.).

How to Gather

When hunting for edible mushrooms to use in the kitchen, pick only the young shaggy manes, the ones with more rounded caps and no sign of decomposing. You can pinch the stem with your fingers, as it should come away quite easily. Handle it carefully, as these mushrooms tend to be quite fragile!

How to Prepare

Unless you plan to use this mushroom as a source of ink, you must cook it within a few hours after picking it. You can saute or bake them and then store them in the refrigerator or freezer. But be warned, even when stored this way, the mushrooms will turn into that gooey sludge within a few days—eat them fast (Kitsteiner, 2022)!

Toss them in stir-fry or fry them up alongside other vegetables. They also work well as meat substitutes in cheesy dishes, pasta, or stuffed mushroom recipes.

Nutritional Content/ Benefits

Shaggy manes provide a host of health benefits: they can boost your immune system and keep your body functioning well due to their high levels of antioxidants (*Learn about the Benefits of Mushroom Blends*, n.d.).

Shaggy mane mushrooms can be a veggie replacement in dishes like these baked parmesan sticks, normally baked with zucchini.

Baked Parmesan Shaggy Mane Sticks

Ingredients:

- 1.5 lb sliced shaggy mane mushrooms
- 3 tbsp olive oil
- ¼ cup lemon juice
- ¼ cup grated parmesan
- 3 cloves minced garlic
- 2 tsp thyme
- ⅛ tsp oregano
- ⅛ tsp salt
- ⅛ tsp pepper

Instructions:

1. Place the sliced mushrooms on the baking tray and drizzle them with olive oil and lemon juice.
2. Add the minced garlic cloves, spreading them evenly over the slices. Sprinkle over all the seasonings.
3. Bake the sticks uncovered on 375F for 15-20 minutes until the sticks have slightly browned and are easy to pierce with a fork.
4. Serve and enjoy!

Adapted from (*Baked Parmesan Mushrooms*, 2014).

Shaggy manes can sometimes be confused with the slightly toxic common inky cap, which also drips a gooey ink and dissolves into an inky puddle. The main difference is that the common inky cap has a completely smooth cap, as opposed to the shaggy mane's scaly texture.

The common inky cap is sometimes edible but can be toxic when it's consumed within a day of drinking alcohol. When this mushroom and alcohol mix, it causes diarrhea, tingling, and vomiting that can be extremely uncomfortable (*The Inky Cap Mushroom: Can You Safely Eat and Consume alcohol?*, 2021).

One or two people have also reported these symptoms when mixing the shaggy mane and alcohol, but this hasn't been revealed to be a common issue. Even so, be cautious when mixing alcohol and shaggy manes, even if it's been several hours since you had a drink (Kitsteiner, 2022)!

Slippery Jack (Suillus luteus)

You either love slippery jack, or you hate slippery jack. This mushroom is a slimy red-brown fungus that looks like a living pile of mud as its most "slippery," but has also earned the nickname "sticky bun" mushroom due to how the slime can sometimes make them look like a yummy cinnamon bun!.

How to Identify

The cap of the slippery jack is a brown or brown-red color and tends to be covered in a shiny, slimy layer of ooze. They're usually bell-shaped when young and grow flatter with age. The underside of the mushroom is light yellow-brown, spongy, and porous.

In the early stages of growth, the underside is covered by a white veil, which gradually descends to make a ring of flesh around the stem. At this stage, you should see brown spots on the white stem above the ring and a brown-purple-colored stem below the ring.

Habitat

Although they especially feature in fall landscapes, you can start looking for slippery jack mushrooms at the end of the Midwestern summer after a good rain shower (Bergo, n.d.-d).

Search around pine trees, especially the red or Norway pine and the eastern white pine. Where these grow, you'll often find other slimy-cap mushrooms (Kuo, 2004).

How to Gather

Use your fingers to pinch and pick small, young slippery jacks, which tend to be less slimy and more appetizing.

How to Prepare

When you cook with slippery jacks, you must start with the painstaking task of trimming or peeling away the slippery top skin and the porous underside, which can cause stomach upset if eaten. You can use the flesh inside the stem and cap, however. You should dry these mushrooms and store them for later use to extend their rather short shelf life (Bergo, n.d.-d).

After this vital step, you can rehydrate and use slippery jacks in dozens of ways—sautee them in butter and garlic, marinate and grill them up, boil them to make a mushroom soup, incorporate them into an omelet, or add them to a pasta or meat dish.

Nutritional Content/ Benefits

These mushrooms provide plenty of protein but are low on fat and carbohydrates. They also contain high levels of vitamin C, iron, zinc, and magnesium, which boost your immune system and provide you with energy (*Natural Product, Slippery Jack*, 2006)!

Correctly prepared slippery jacks exude an earthy, woody smell and taste that adds a lovely flavor to lots of dishes.

Slippery Jack Mushroom Rub

Ingredients:

- ½ cup dried slippery jack mushrooms
- 1 tsp onion powder
- ½ tsp garlic powder
- 1 tsp dried thyme
- 1 tsp paprika
- ½ tsp salt

Instructions:

1. Grind the dried mushrooms in a coffee grinder or blender.
2. Mix the ground mushrooms with the other spices.
3. Store the rub in a container until you're ready to rub it onto steak or meat.
4. Enjoy!

Adapted from (*Slippery Jack Mushroom-Coffee Rub*, n.d.).

WARNING

Slippery jack's lookalikes are usually other slimy-capped mushrooms, which aren't toxic. However, you must always carefully identify any mushroom you find and plan to eat.

Smooth Chanterelle
(Cantharellus lateritius)

Smooth chanterelles are the giants of the chanterelle family, providing plenty of edible material for foragers looking for mushrooms to cook with! This massive Midwestern mushroom is perfect for light summer meals and absolutely perfect for beginners to hunt.

How to Identify

Smooth chanterelle mushrooms have features similar to other chanterelles, such as the yellow foot chanterelle. It's trumpet-shaped, with a wavy edge that sometimes bunches up to resemble a bright yellow flower.

The color on the inside is bright orange or orange-yellow, and the underside tends to be a paler orange-yellow. The underside of the wavy cap has some light ridges. These mushrooms tend to grow in tight clusters, meeting at their white stems (*Smooth Chanterelle*, n.d.).

Habitat

These are summer mushrooms, appearing from the end of June to the beginning of August. Search for them in forests populated with oaks and hickories. Intrepid foragers can look for them on mossy beds deep in the woods, while beginners can search in the grass and leaves along paths and hiking trails (*Smooth Chanterelle*, n.d.).

How to Gather

Pinch and twist to pull up smaller smooth chanterelles, or use your knife to cut away larger ones.

How to Prepare

After rinsing out the dirt that often gets trapped in the cup of this mushroom, pat it dry and decide what you want to do next. You can dry and store them or use them quickly. Saute them in pasta sauces or as a buttery side dish, cut up and bake them into tarts, or boil these chanterelles as part of an earthy soup!

Nutritional Content/ Benefits

These healthful mushrooms can boost your immune system, bone strength, and moods with their high levels of vitamin D, vitamin A, potassium, and phosphorus. There are plenty more vitamins and minerals in these mushrooms that are great for your body, so eat plenty of these delicious fungi (Brennan, 2020)!

RECIPE/REMEDY

Fruity, smooth chanterelles are great in pasta dishes like risotto and pasta alfredo!

Chanterelle Risotto

Ingredients:

- 4 tbsp butter
- 1 small minced onion
- ⅛ tsp salt
- 2 cloves minced garlic
- ½ lb diced chanterelle mushrooms
- 2 cups risotto
- ½ cup white wine
- 1 tsp thyme
- 6 cups vegetable stock
- 1 cup sweet corn
- ¼ cup grated cheese

Instructions:

1. Heat the butter in a pan over medium heat. Add the onions and cook until they turn translucent. Sprinkle with salt, then add the mushrooms. Cook the mushrooms until they soften. Add the garlic and cook for another 30 seconds until fragrant.
2. In another pot, begin heating the vegetable stock.
3. Add a bit more butter and then rice. Stir the rice into the other ingredients and cook for a few minutes until the rice becomes translucent.
4. Pour in the white wine and stir the rice until the rice becomes tender. Slowly add the vegetable stock a scoop at a time and keep stirring well.
5. Once the rice is cooked and the soup is hot, add the sweet corn and cook for another minute or two.
6. Remove the dish from the stove. Sprinkle the cheese over the dish.
7. Serve and enjoy!

Adapted from (*Shaw*, 2017).

Look out for the common chanterelle lookalikes, especially the jack-o'-lantern mushroom. Some hints that can help you discern these mushrooms are the color, size, and gills. Jack-o'-lantern mushrooms are a duller color, possess true gills, and tend to grow much smaller than the gigantic, vibrant, smooth chanterelles (Adamant, 2018). Always take the time to identify any chanterelle you find!

Omphalotus olearius.

Tawny Milkcap (Lactifluus volemus)

If you're looking for the ideal picturesque summer mushroom, look no farther than the lovely tawny milkcap. As its name suggests, it secretes a milky fluid within the gills when it's cut, but surprisingly, it smells just like fish! Thankfully, after cooking it up, the mushroom has a delicious, milder taste that's popular in culinary circles.

How to Identify

The cap of the tawny milkcap in the Midwest is a light honey brown or reddish-brown with a deep divot in the center. The white or brown gills are tightly packed and touch the top of the stem.

The stem itself is slightly ridged and relatively thick, colored in shades of white and brown. The edges of the cap tend to hang down slightly when young and turn upwards with age, sometimes even forming a cup shape.

Habitat

Tawny milkcaps appear all through the summer. Look for these mushrooms in Midwestern forests with hardwoods, beech trees, and conifers. If you find any chanterelles, look nearby—you might be able to spot some tawny milkcaps, too (Bergo, n.d.-c).

How to Gather

Pinch the mushroom at the base where it meets the ground, and twist to pull it away.

How to Prepare

When you cut this mushroom, expect to see some brown bruising or staining. You can store the mushrooms whole by submerging them in a bowl of salt water for a day, but it's a good idea to use these mushrooms quickly after picking them (*Uses of Tawny Milkcap*, n.d.).

Simply toasting or sauteing these mushrooms brings out their delicious nutty flavor. They can also be used on top of pizzas or salads when sliced or tossed into pasta sauces, similar to the way button mushrooms are used. The milky secretion makes them a great candidate for use in stews and casseroles since it will thicken these dishes.

Nutritional Content/ Benefits

More research is needed to determine the nutrients these mushrooms deliver to humans, but rest assured that tawny milkycaps provide necessary vitamins and minerals that contribute towards overall health, just like all mushrooms!

You can enjoy the nutty flavor of these mushrooms to the fullest in this delicious recipe!

Slow Cooker Tawny Milkcap Chili

Ingredients:

- 1 tbsp olive oil
- 1 small chopped white onion
- 1 chopped green bell pepper
- 2 minced garlic cloves
- 2 cups chopped tawny milkcap mushrooms
- 1 can diced tomatoes
- 1 tsp cocoa powder
- 1 tsp paprika
- 1 tsp cumin
- 1 tsp oregano
- ½ tsp thyme
- ¼ tsp black pepper
- 1 tsp salt
- 4 cups vegetable broth
- 1 can garbanzo beans
- 1 can red beans
- Sour cream
- 1 bag Mexican shredded cheese

Instructions:

1. In a pan over medium heat, heat oil and add onions. Cook until translucent. Add mushrooms and cook for a few minutes until they soften, then add the garlic for 30 seconds until fragrant.
2. Add the pan contents and all the ingredients except the sour cream and shredded cheese to the slow cooker. Stir everything until well combined.
3. Cook on low heat for 5-6 hours and on high heat for 3-4 hours.
4. Dish out and top with sour cream and shredded cheese.
5. Enjoy!

Adapted from (*Sanchez*, 2017).

WARNING

Although tawny milkcap is fairly unique, be cautious of mushrooms that secrete milky moisture like the tawny milkcap. Some mushrooms with this same feature can be toxic. Always carefully identify any mushroom you plan to eat!

Veiled Oyster (Pleurotus dryinus)

The veiled oyster looks like a creature that belongs in the ocean rather than the forest. With its white, gently arching, shelf-like cap, this mushroom truly resembles an oyster's top shell; when viewed from below, the curvy central gills can cause it to look like a jellyfish swimming through the forest.

How to Identify

Veiled oysters are another type of shelf-like mushrooms that grow straight out of tree trunks. They feature flat or gently curved white caps, with a partial skirt-like veil hanging around the outer edge. The mushrooms are medium to large, about 13 centimeters in diameter at the largest.

The deep white gills are easily seen running down into a ring on the stem or right into the tree. If you've found a mushroom with the ring below it, you'll see an off-white, smooth stem set into the tree or log (Kummer, 2020).

Habitat

In this region, veiled oysters appear all throughout the summer and fall. Search the trunks of oaks, beeches, and other hardwood trees growing in Midwestern forests, as on recently dead trees or rotting hardwood logs and stumps (Kuo, 2018).

How to Gather

Choose smaller, younger, more tender mushrooms for an easier cooking and eating experience. Use your knife to cut the stem and cap away from the wood where it grows.

How to Prepare

These mushrooms are exceedingly popular in dishes all over the world. They can be sauteed, fried, boiled, or baked in a variety of tasty dishes, similar to how the regular oyster mushroom can be used.

Nutritional Content/ Benefits

This mushroom has not had much independent study with regards to its nutritional benefit, but it's most likely close in nutritional content to its family member, the oyster mushroom.

Young mushrooms bring a citrusy smell and tender taste to meals they're added to!

Braised Veiled Oysters

Ingredients:

- 2 tbsp olive oil
- 1 chopped shallot
- 1.5 tsp salt
- 3-5 chopped veiled oyster mushrooms
- 1.5 tsp thyme
- 2 tbsp white wine or sherry
- ½ cup vegetable broth
- 1 tbsp cornstarch

Instructions:

1. Heat the oil in a pan over medium heat. Toss in the chopped shallots and sprinkle with ¾ tsp salt. Cook until the shallots become tender.
2. Add in the chopped mushrooms and the other ¾ tsp salt. Cook the mushrooms until the liquid dissipates and they begin to brown and slightly caramelize.
3. Pour in the sherry/white wine and the broth. Sprinkle in the thyme. Turn down the heat to low. Stir this mixture occasionally while continuing to heat.
4. Wait until the liquid reduces, then turn up the heat until only half the liquid is left.
5. Mix 1 tbsp of cornstarch with 1 tbsp of cornstarch, then stir until the sauce thickens.
6. Serve and enjoy!

Adapted from (*De Laurentiis*, 2022).

WARNING

This thick white shelf-like mushroom has one potential toxic lookalike in the deadly angel wing, or *Pleurocybella porrigens*, mushroom. However, angel wings tend to grow on conifer trees and are much thinner than veiled oysters. Angel wings are also more spoon-shaped than the veiled oyster (Haritan, n.d.). Therefore, you must always carefully identify any and all mushrooms you plant to make a meal out of.

Pleurocybella porrigens.

Chapter 7:

Filling Fall Mushrooms

Chicken of the Woods
(Laetiprous sulphreus)

This brown and yellow shelf mushroom looks mouthwatering even before you pick them from the trees where they grow. Depending on their coloring and patterns, they can look like slices of fried chicken or a stack of crispy fried pancakes.

How to Identify

Chicken of the woods are fan-shaped mushrooms that grow directly from trees, with only a small partial stem growing from the underside. The top is orange or yellow, and the edges are wavy with a yellow stripe. The porous underside is typically yellow or white (Smola, 2020).

Habitat

Chicken of the woods appear in late summer and last through the fall. Look for them growing in clusters or piles on dead, dying, or injured trees, especially on oak trees and other hardwoods. They can also be found on the occasional live tree (*Chicken of the Woods*, n.d.).

How to Gather

Harvest some of the mushrooms that you can reach by cutting the stem and cap where it sprouts from the tree!

How to Prepare

Trim away the stem, which tends to be tough and dirty, and wash away the dirt that gets trapped in the cap. Quickly rinse off the mushroom if necessary, but quickly dry it unless you want a soggy mushroom.

You can cook them right away and then freeze any mushrooms you don't plan to eat, which is the best way to preserve these edible fungi. You can saute, make, or fry them up in recipes that call for meat since these mushrooms taste like lemony chicken (Windish, 2018).

Nutritional Content/ Benefits

Enjoy these mushrooms without guilt since they have low carbs and low fat. However, they pack a punch nutritionally, providing your body with vitamin A, vitamin C, potassium, and protein (Smola, 2020). Your immune system will thank you!

RECIPE/REMEDY

This recipe is a great example of how chicken of the woods can be used as a meaty replacement for chicken in tons of familiar recipes!

Buffalo Chicken of the Woods

Ingredients:

- 1.5 lb chicken of the woods
- 3 tbsp butter
- ⅓ cup hot sauce
- 1 clove minced garlic
- 1 tbsp olive oil

Instructions:

1. Slice your mushrooms into "chicken strip"-sized pieces.
2. Place them on a baking sheet covered with parchment paper, drizzle them in olive oil, and bake them in the oven at 400F for 15-20 minutes.
3. In a pan on medium heat, melt the butter. Toss in the garlic and cook for 30 seconds until the garlic is fragrant. Pour in the hot sauce and stir to mix the melted butter and hot sauce.
4. Add the crispy mushrooms straight from the oven. Toss them in the hot sauce and sprinkle them with salt and pepper to taste.
5. Serve and enjoy!

Adapted from (*Jacob*, n.d.).

WARNING

This mushroom has no toxic lookalikes, but always identify any mushroom you forage and plan to eat.

Elm Oyster (Hypsizygus ulmarius)

The elm oyster is another shelf-like mushroom and member of the oyster mushroom family, although this variety can grow to huge heights and sprout out of most foragers' reach on towering tree trunks.

How to Identify

The elm oyster's cap is white or tan, flat or slightly rounded. It can grow up to 15 centimeters in diameter. It has a thick stem that can also grow quite long, about 10 centimeters, sometimes forming a curve between the tree and the cap.

The elm oyster features a clear distinction between where the stem begins and the closely-packed gills end, which is how you can distinguish this oyster mushroom from others in its family (*Elm Oyster | Hypsizygus Ulmarius*, n.d.).

Habitat

Elm oysters grow through all the months of fall, from August to December. Travel to the forests around the Midwest where deciduous trees grow and look up into the elm, beech, maple, and oak trees to find elm oysters. These mushrooms especially love box elder maples, so finding one of these trees increases your chances of finding this tasty mushroom (Nelson, n.d.).

How to Gather

Use your pocket knife to cut the long stem of whatever elm oysters you can reach. Although some might grow quite far up the tree, leave them alone unless you have a safe way to reach them!

How to Prepare

Keep the stem on these mushrooms, but gently wipe or trim away any dirty parts. Keep in mind that the stem will be tough, and the mushrooms are filled with moisture, so cook them until the stems become tender, and the liquid dissipates.

This mushroom is infinitely edible. Delectable elm oysters can be fried, sauteed, boiled, and roasted (*Elm Oyster Mushrooms*, 2013). You can even dry them and grind them into a flavorful powder which you can add to soups, stews, and broths!

Nutritional Content/ Benefits

Elm oysters provide a host of benefits, including high levels of vitamin D and protein that give you energy and boost your mood (*Elm Oyster Mushrooms*, 2013).

RECIPE/REMEDY

These mushrooms have a nice, mild flavor that works well in other flavorful dishes.

Herby Fried Elm Oysters

Ingredients:

- 2 tbsp olive oil
- 1.5 cups elm oyster mushrooms
- 3 crushed garlic cloves
- ½ tsp thyme
- ½ tsp oregano
- 2 tbsp unsalted butter
- ½ tsp lemon juice
- ⅛ tsp salt
- ⅛ tsp pepper

Instructions:

1. Heat the oil in a pan over medium heat. Add the oyster mushrooms and cook until the liquid dissipates and the mushrooms brown.
2. Add the crushed garlic cloves and cook for another 30 seconds, until fragrant.
3. Add the butter and sprinkle the thyme and oregano over the mushrooms. Continue to cook everything for several minutes on low heat, coating the mushrooms well in the butter and thyme.
4. Wait for the mushrooms to turn a dark brown before taking them off the heat. Add the lemon juice, salt, and pepper.
5. Serve!

Adapted from (*Pan Fried Oyster Mushrooms*, 2019).

You might accidentally confuse the elm oyster with the similar-looking ivory funnel mushroom or *Clitocybe dealbata*. Both are white and flat, with a clear distinction between the gills and stem. However, the ivory funnel's stem is located in the middle of the cap, while the elm oyster's stem is off-center and quite a bit larger. Ivory funnels also grow from the ground, while elm oysters grow from trees.

Ivory funnels can be quite dangerous, inducing symptoms like stomach pain, blurred vision, and difficulty breathing, so carefully identify elm oysters before packing them in your bag or basket (*7 Types of Oyster Mushrooms & 3 Poisonous Look-Alikes*, 2020).

Clitocybe dealbata.

Enoki, Velvet Shank
(Flammulina velutipes)

If you've ever gone to an authentic East Asian restaurant or eaten authentic cuisine, you've probably seen enoki mushrooms floating in soups, included in rice dishes, or wrapped in beef.

How to Identify

Velvet shank caps are burnt orange-red with a shiny sheen that makes them look like they're made of rubber. Expect the caps to be anywhere from 1 to 7 centimeters across. These rounded caps have white or yellow gills underneath, and the gills are of varying lengths.

The gills touch the dark red or black stem, which is set in the middle of the cap. The stem is long and often curved to accommodate the mushroom as it sprouts from trees and wood pieces.

Habitat

Velvet shanks grow from October to May, so you can search for them all through the fall. You can find clusters of these mushrooms growing on pieces of wood—even if they appear to be growing from grass, they're really growing from a buried log or stump. Look particularly around hardwood trees in forests all over the Midwest (Kuo, 2013).

How to Gather

Pinch and twist or cut the stem of the mushroom where it sprouts from the wood. If you're a culinary forager, look for small, young velvet shanks that are more tender and delicious.

How to Prepare

You must remove the shiny skin on top of the mushroom before eating it, so carefully trim or peel this layer away. You can use the rest of the mushroom in a variety of recipes, from stir-fry to sauteed snacks. Experiment using velvet shank in recipes that call for the cultivated enoki rolls, like East Asian-inspired soups and rice dishes!

Nutritional Content/ Benefits

Wild velvet shank contains vitamin B's and other essential vitamins and minerals that boost your immune system and reduce inflammation (*Nutrition – Nature's Way*, n.d.).

While this dish is usually made with cultivated enoki mushrooms, you can also make it with your wild harvested velvet shanks!

Grilled Beef-Wrapped Velvet Shank

Ingredients:

- 100 g thinly sliced beef brisket
- ⅛ tsp black pepper
- ½ cup thinly sliced velvet shanks
- 2 tbsp butter
- 1 tbsp light soy sauce
- 1 tsp sesame oil
- 1 tbsp rice wine
- 1 tsp brown sugar
- ¼ tsp cornstarch

Instructions:

1. Set the thin slices of beef on a cutting board and sprinkle the pepper over each beef piece. Within each slice, place a bunch of sliced velvet shanks perpendicular to the beef. Wrap the shanks in the beef and hold in place with a toothpick.
2. In a bowl, mix together the soy sauce, sesame oil, rice wine, brown sugar, and black pepper. Mix together ¼ tsp cornstarch and ¼ tsp water, and whisk this mixture into the sauce.
3. In a pan on the stove, add the butter and let it melt on medium heat. Place the beef rolls in the pan. Cook them until they're brown on each side.
4. Pour the sauce over the wraps and let the rolls simmer for a minute or two until the sauce reduces slightly.
5. Serve and enjoy!

Adapted from (*Spice N' Pans*, 2018).

Be careful not to confuse this mushroom with the funeral bell mushroom, *Galerina marginata*, which can be deadly if eaten. Look closely at the stem, which usually features a ring of flesh; the cap of the funeral bell sometimes has the remnants of a veil, as well (*Velvet Shank, Flammulina Velutipes*, n.d.).

Galerina marginata.

Giant Puffball
(Calvatia gigantea)

Pillowy giant puffballs are a treat for Midwestern foragers. These monstrous mushrooms are often mistaken for volleyballs or soccer balls lying in the grass, so keep your eyes peeled on your foraging trips!

How to Identify

Giant puffballs are white, rounded mushrooms that have no stem. They grow almost perfectly round but can sometimes be a bit irregular. The outside of the mushrooms is fairly smooth, although don't be surprised to notice some cracking or cratering in older mushrooms.

The biggest indication that you've found a giant puffball is the flesh inside, which is entirely smooth and white (*Giant Puffball*, n.d.).

Habitat

Begin the hunt for these delightful mushrooms in August, and keep searching through October. Keep your eyes out for these mushrooms as you stroll through the prairies, golf courses, pastures, and lawns of the Midwest. They mostly grow directly from these grassy areas, but they sometimes sprout up on deciduous forest floors, as well (*Giant Puffball*, n.d.).

How to Gather

Culinary foragers should seek out smaller, more fluffy giant puff-balls that feel marshmallowy to the touch. You can simply pull up this mushroom, as there's no stem attaching it to the ground, only mycelium. Cut off a piece of the mushroom to confirm that it's completely white with only flesh inside before putting it in your bag, as well as to check for any bugs who might have made a home in the bottom part of your mushroom (Sayner, n.d.).

How to Prepare

If your mushroom is a bit older and the outer skin is tough, peel it away after a quick wipe with a dry cloth or brush. Slice up the mushroom into edible pieces, and then use it as a substitute for meat or vegetables in any number of meals. Bake them with parmesan cheese, fry them in egg and flour, add them on top of a pizza, or saute them up in a spicy stir fry!

Nutritional Content/ Benefits

Giant puffball mushrooms are not only tasty and filling but also low in calories, so you can indulge worry-free! They also offer health benefits such as high protein to keep your body running. These amazing mushrooms can also help to lower cholesterol and boost your immune system (Tjandra, 2019).

RECIPE/REMEDY

Meaty puffballs are great in simple recipes and can surely fill you up!

Garlic-Lemon Sauteed Puffball

Ingredients:

- 3 tbsp butter
- 1 sliced onion
- 4 minced garlic cloves
- ½ tsp salt
- 1 lb diced giant puffball
- ¼ tsp pepper
- Lemon zest and juice
- ¼ cup chopped parsley

Instructions:

1. Melt the butter in a pan over medium heat. Add the sliced onions and cook until they become translucent. Add the minced garlic and salt and cook for another 30 seconds until it's fragrant.
2. Mix in the diced mushroom pieces. Saute them until they're mostly brown, between 5-10 minutes.
3. Add the pepper, lemon zest, and lemon juice and cook for another minute or two until the flavors have incorporated.
4. Take the mixture off the heat and add the parsley.
5. Serve and enjoy!

Adapted from (*Six Delicious Giant Puffball Recipes*, 2016).

WARNING

Small, round, white mushrooms could be giant puffballs, but they could also be young members of the poisonous *Amanita* family. Cut open the "puffball" to see if there is any sign of a stem or cap. If you find these instead of smooth white flesh, toss the mushroom aside and don't eat it—you've probably found the deadly *Amanita bisporigera*, also called the destroying angel mushroom (*Giant Puffball*, n.d.).

Amanita bisporigera.

Golden Oyster Mushroom
(Pleurotus citrinopileatus)

Although they've only quite become part of the North American landscape within the last decade, there are now plenty of these golden, nutty mushrooms out there for you to discover!

How to Identify

Golden oysters are a bright yellow or orange color, standing out vibrantly against the forest landscape. They're shelf mushrooms that sprout from trees and can appear either flat or more trumpet-shaped, with a fairly deep dimple in the middle of the cap and sometimes curled-over edges.

The underside of this mushroom features white or pinkish gills that run in parallel lines all down the stem. This stem is normally attached to other stems in a clustering formation. If you give this mushroom a sniff, it smells quite fruity. These mushrooms are small or medium, with caps usually no larger than 7 centimeters across (Emberger, n.d.).

Habitat

The season of the golden oyster lasts from spring to the early months of fall, so get out there in September and early October, when the weather is still fairly warm.

Golden oysters are saprobic and thrive on dead matter, so you'll find them growing on dead trees, logs, and stumps, typically on hardwood trees. Look for them in Midwestern hardwood forests that contain oaks, elms, and beeches (Emberger, n.d.).

How to Gather

When you find a cluster of these mushrooms, use your pocket knife to cut them away from the tree. You'll pull out a bunch at a time, which makes for low-effort foraging!

How to Prepare

Don't rinse golden oysters with water since they already contain high moisture levels. Brush them off instead. You can store them for a couple of days in an open container in the fridge, but use these mushrooms quickly, or dry and preserve them.

To make a delicious meal, try incorporating them into a stir-fry, adding them into a pasta sauce, baking them in the oven, or simply sauteing them with butter and garlic (*Yellow Oyster Mushrooms Information and Facts*, n.d.). These mushrooms are incredibly versatile in the kitchen, so feel free to experiment and add them to any recipe!

Nutritional Content/ Benefits

Like other oyster mushrooms, golden oysters are packed with vitamins and minerals, including metabolism-boosting zinc, bone-protecting copper, and cell-securing folic acid (*Yellow Oyster Mushrooms Information and Facts*, n.d.).

RECIPE/REMEDY

The delightfully nutty taste of the golden oyster mushroom makes it a prized ingredient in dishes around the world, such as this heavenly pasta.

Creamy Oyster Mushroom Pasta

Ingredients:

- ½ lb pasta of choice
- 3 tbsp unsalted butter
- 1 lb chopped oyster mushrooms
- 3 minced garlic cloves
- ½ tsp salt
- ½ tsp black pepper
- ½ cup heavy cream
- ¼ cup chopped parsley
- ¼ cup parmesan cheese

Instructions:

1. In a pot of water on high heat, boil the pasta.
2. In a pan over medium heat, melt the butter. Add the chopped mushrooms and saute them for several minutes until they brown. Then toss in the garlic and cook them for about 30 seconds until they're fragrant.
3. Sprinkle the salt and pepper over the mushrooms and garlic. Pour in the heavy cream and keep on medium heat until the cream reduces slightly, stirring occasionally.
4. Take off the heat, then sprinkle parsley and parmesan cheese over the dish.
5. Serve and enjoy!

Adapted from (*Oyster Mushroom Pasta With A Creamy Sauce*, 2021).

Due to their orange-ish color and somewhat similar habitat, golden oyster mushrooms might be confused for the poisonous jack-o'-lantern mushroom. But observe the color very closely. Jack-o'-lanterns, as their name suggests, are more pumpkin-colored, while golden oysters are more of a yellow or yellow-tinged golden color (Carlin, 2020).

You can also take a look at the shape and formation. Jack-o'-lanterns are typically somewhat rounded and bunched with clear individual stems, while golden oysters grow flatter and in clusters with connected stems (Featherstone, 2021).

Omphalotus olearius.

Hen of the Woods (Grifola frondosa)

Hen of the woods are fantastic fall fungi that look like they belong to autumn, with their dark brown coloring and appearance similar to a pile of fallen leaves. However, this also means that foragers need eagle eyes to pick these mushrooms out in the fall landscape!

How to Identify

Hen of the woods consists of multiple caps that make up one gigantic cluster. The caps are dark gray-brown and are either fan- or cup-shaped. The underside of each cap is white and porous and runs down to the tiny whitish stem, which links each individual cap to the cluster-at-large.

Rather than a stem, the cluster has a small underground tuber that's easily pulled up, similar to the giant puffball mushroom. The clusters can grow huge, sometimes 60 centimeters across and up to 100 pounds (*Grifola Frondosa – Midwest American Mycological Information*, n.d.).

Habitat

Hen of the woods almost exclusively appears in the fall, when the weather begins to turn cold. Search for them from September to November (*Hen of the Woods*, n.d.).

These mushrooms thrive by taking nutrients from trees, so

look for them on dead or dying oaks and the occasional maple. You can find them deep in forests or in local parks and lawns. They don't grow high up on the tree trunk but rather at the bottom, which can contribute to their camouflage as a simple pile of leaves.

How to Gather

Look for the smaller specimens of hen of the woods, which will be more tender and edible and much easier to clean (Bergo, n.d.). Cut the cluster away from the tree, but leave a bit on the tree so you can return again next season for more.

How to Prepare

These mushrooms require quite a bit of cleaning and preparation, but they're so delicious that it's worth it. You'll need to carefully clean out the fallen leaves, acorns, twigs, and even various bugs from the cluster. Cook them up quickly and then store them in the freezer for later; make them fresh in the dish of your choice, or dry them and store them in a container.

Before cooking, cut it up into smaller pieces (including the stem) and use them in almost any recipe you can imagine. They're delicious roasted, grilled, sauteed, boiled, pickled, or baked. Add them to soups, sauces, pasta dishes, meaty entrees, or breakfast dishes. You can even dry these mushrooms and grind them into a flavorful powder that's easy to preserve and use year-round (Bergo, n.d.-b).

Nutritional Content/ Benefits

Hen of the woods is wonderful for boosting your immune system. If you're feeling stressed, eating some hen of the woods can keep your immune system running well (*Grifola Frondosa – Midwest American Mycological Information*, n.d.).

These delightfully crunchy mushrooms make a delicious addition to any autumn feast!

Grilled Sesame Hen of the Woods

Ingredients:

- 2 lb sliced hen of the woods mushrooms
- 2 tbsp sesame oil
- 1 tbsp toasted sesame seeds
- Salt and pepper(to taste)
- 2 tbsp basil
- 1 tsp lime juice

Instructions:

1. Set out the hen of the woods mushrooms. Use a brush to coat the mushrooms on all sides with sesame oil and sprinkle them with salt and pepper.
2. Grill the mushrooms on an indoor or outdoor grill, flipping on both sides until the mushroom has browned and become slightly crunchy.
3. Sprinkle the mushrooms with the toasted sesame seeds and basil, and drip some lime juice over the mushrooms.
4. Serve and enjoy!

Adapted from (*Vongerichten*, n.d.).

WARNING

Hen of the woods has no toxic lookalikes, but you must always carefully identify each mushroom you plan to eat.

Honey Mushroom (Armillaria mellea)

Honey mushrooms grow in abundance wherever they can be found, which is great news for foragers who love using these mushrooms in the kitchen.

How to Identify

Young honey mushrooms look wildly different from older honey mushrooms. Younger mushrooms have small, sticky, yellow caps covered in a pollen-like substance. Older mushrooms feature tawny brown, flattened caps with hints of yellow.

No matter what its cap looks like, they always have black hairs sprouting from the middle of the cap. Older mushrooms have a distinct ring of flesh around the top of the stem. But if you've found the rounded yellow cap, this ring will still be a veil that covers the gills.

The gills of this mushroom are white, turning a bit darker as time passes. The white stems are usually fused together, so you'll typically find these mushrooms growing in flower bouquet-like clusters (*Honey Mushroom*, n.d.).

Habitat

These mushrooms crop up between August and November. You can find them sprouting close to dead and dying oak trees, wherever these trees can be found. They tend to cluster around the bottom of the tree's trunk or stump. Some honey mushrooms might also appear to grow from the grass on top of buried pieces of wood (*Honey Mushroom*, n.d.).

How to Gather

Cut away the smaller mushrooms in the area with your pocket knife, or pinch and twist the stem to pluck them. Remember, the smaller, the better when it comes to cooking them!

How to Prepare

Before you begin your culinary experiments, brush away any dirt and separate the caps from the stems, as the caps are much more edible. If you don't plan to use them immediately, you can boil them and then freeze them or dry and store them.

You'll need to cook these mushrooms longer than your intuition might suggest, so add a few extra minutes to the cooking time in whatever recipe you're using, from soups to casseroles to stuffings to flavored butters.

These mushrooms are amazing additions to sauces and soups that require a thickening agent since their natural sweet secretions do this on their own. For other recipes, consider soaking them in salt water to dry up this edible slime (Bergo, n.d.-c).

Nutritional Content/ Benefits

The zinc, copper, and iron in these delicious mushrooms can contribute to your overall health, giving you energy and protecting your heart (Lixandru, 2019).

Honey mushrooms are a sweet addition to these crispy fried dumplings!

Pan-Fried Honey Mushroom Dumplings

Ingredients:

- Pack of dumpling wrappers
- 2 tbsp oil
- 1.4 tbsp minced ginger
- 4 cloves minced garlic
- 1 cup chopped bamboo shoots
- 3.5 cups minced honey mushrooms
- 1 cup diced tofu
- ¼ tsp salt
- 1 tbsp cooking wine or sherry
- 1 tbsp soy sauce
- 2 tbsp nutritional yeast
- 1 tsp sesame oil

Instructions:

1. Set out the dumpling wrappers and a large bowl.
2. Heat the oil in a pan over medium heat, and then cook the ginger and garlic until they become fragrant.
3. Toss in the bamboo shoots, tofu, mushrooms, and salt. Stir and cook until all the liquid dissipates.
4. Add the wine or sherry and wait until that liquid is gone.
5. Put the mixture into the waiting bowl and mix in the rest of the ingredients until everything is well-combined.
6. Scoop an equal amount of filling into each wrap. Fold the wrapper in half and pinch the edge closed with a slightly wet finger.
7. Pan-fry the dumplings by heating oil in the pan over hot heat and flipping the dumplings once each side has browned.
8. Serve and enjoy!

Adapted from (*Mushroom Dumplings*, 2019).

Be careful not to confuse the honey mushroom with the deadly funeral bell, *Galerina marginata*. The latter can cause dangerous poisoning symptoms, sometimes even leading to kidney failure.

Funeral bells won't be clustered like honey mushrooms tend to be, and the gills of the funeral bell are a dark red-brown. Take a spore print if you're unsure about your foraged mushroom's identity. The edible honey mushroom has white or pale yellow spores, but the funeral bell has red-brown spores (*Honey Mushroom & Deadly Galerina — Identification and Differences*, n.d.).

Galerina marginata.

Indigo Milk Cap (Lactarius indigo)

Bring your camera when you're on the hunt for these mushrooms since odds are you'll want to capture the beauty of these blue fungi in their natural habitat!

How to Identify

Young indigo milk caps are an intense, vibrant blue, although older mushrooms turn a shade of green and gray. The cap's shape ranges from deeply rounded to cup-shaped. The stem becomes hollow as the mushroom ages, and the spores are off-white.

The closely-packed gills run from the cap's edge to meet the stem and are vibrant indigo. The stem, meanwhile, is white on the outside, although the places of the stem where you cut will turn the same indigo blue.

Like other milk caps, you'll see a blue or dark green milky substance leaking from the cut when you scrape or cut the gills. Any bruises on the mushroom will be green (*Indigo Milky*, n.d.).

Habitat

Indigo milk caps appear in the hottest weather and last from mid-summer to mid-autumn, from around July to October. Search hardwood and coniferous forests for spots of bright blue around the base of oak and pine trees (*Indigo Milky*, n.d.).

How to Gather

Pluck these mushrooms by pinching the stem and twisting it. Give it a brush to remove dirt and scatter some spores around the area.

How to Prepare

Clean the mushroom with a brush, especially getting into the gills. Cook them up quickly or dry and preserve them for later use.

These are great mushrooms to experiment with due to their versatility. Fry them up alongside other veggies, blend them into salad dressings, or cook them lightly in scrambled eggs to make a meal straight out of a Dr. Seuss book (von Frank, 2014)!

Cooking for long periods of time drains the blue from the mushroom, so it can be a puzzle to figure out how to prepare these mushrooms while preserving their bright indigo color (Bergo, n.d.-e).

Nutritional Content/ Benefits

Eating these mushrooms gives you plenty of fiber and protein, which is good for your digestive system and energy levels (Saunders, 2021).

Using indigo milk caps in this vinaigrette means that you can have a delicious salad dressing that's dyed a bright natural blue!

Indigo Milk Cap Vinaigrette

Ingredients:

- 1 cup vegetable broth
- 3 cups chopped indigo milky caps
- ⅓ cup olive oil
- ⅓ cup white wine vinegar
- 1 minced garlic clove
- 1 tbsp diced shallot
- 1 tbsp thyme
- 1 tsp salt
- ¼ tsp pepper

Instructions:

1. Combine the mushrooms, vinegar, garlic, shallot, thyme, salt, and pepper in a bowl. Let it sit for several minutes, so the mushrooms absorb the vinegar well.
2. Pour the contents of the bowl into a blender. Slowly add vegetable broth as you blend the mixture until it's smooth.
3. Add the remaining oil, then blend for another few seconds until well-mixed.
4. Pour the blended vinaigrette into a sealable salad dressing container and keep it in the fridge or freezer for when you're ready to use.
5. Enjoy!

Adapted from (*Bergo*, n.d.-e).

The dark blue coloring and blue milky "blood" of these mushrooms make them unique in the Midwestern landscape, but you might mistake them for poisonous members of the *Cortinarius* family. Instead, cut the mushroom to observe the color that leaks out since *Cortinarius* mushrooms don't secrete any fluid when cut (von Frank, 2014). Always double-check the identity of each blue mushroom you forage for eating!

Cortinarius violaceus.

Lion's Mane (Hericium erinaceus)

Even during the fall, you can find some faux icicles in the forests of the Midwest—the remarkable lion's mane mushroom appears to be a clump of falling hair or a bunch of spiky icicles hanging from a tree.

How to Identify

These striking mushrooms are simple to identify. Simply look for their long, white strands or spikes of fungal matter, which are usually about 5 centimeters long. All these strands are attached to a white stem that's usually hidden from view but attaches the mushroom to the wood from which it grows.

Habitat

Begin the hunt for these unique mushrooms in cooler weather, from the end of summer through the fall. Start your hunt for these lion's manes in mixed and hardwood forests around the Midwest. Since these mushrooms get nutrients from dead or dying trees, look around oak, beech, maple logs, stumps, or rotting trees (Goetzman, 2018).

How to Gather

Use your pocket knife to cut the cluster of lion's mane away from the tree. Do your best to brush as much dirt as possible from the clustered strands.

How to Prepare

Rinse the "hair" of the lion's mane with water and trim away any parts that are still dirty. They'll stay fresh in the fridge for about a week if you keep them in a breathable container like a paper bag.

You can cut up the mushroom, stem and all, into slices of mushroom that you can fry, sautee, or add to soup. Lion's mane makes a good substitute for seafood in dishes since it tastes vaguely like crab (Goetzman, 2018).

Nutritional Content/ Benefits

People with Arthritis and anyone suffering from inflammation can benefit from eating lion's mane, which has anti-inflammatory properties (Julson, 2018).

Slow Cooker Lion's Mane Steaks

Ingredients:

- 1 lb lion's mane mushrooms
- 3 cups vegetable stock
- ¼ cup steak seasoning
- 1 tbsp Worcestershire sauce

Instructions:

1. Cut the mushrooms into steak strips.
2. Place the mushroom pieces in a slow cooker. Pour over a mixture of the vegetable stock, seasoning, and Worcestershire sauce.
3. Let the mushrooms cook for 1 or 2 hours on high or 3-4 hours on low.
4. Serve and enjoy!

Adapted from (*Thompson*, 2020).

WARNING

There are no mushrooms that look like the lion's mane, but as always, confirm the identity of any mushroom before eating it.

Lobster Mushroom
(Hypomyces lactifluorum)

The lobster mushroom gets its name from its red-orange crust, which sometimes cracks to reveal the tender white flesh underneath—very much like a lobster of the forest!

How to Identify

Funnel-shaped lobster mushrooms are bright orange-red, with wavy or folded edges. The bumpy outside of the funnel has short ribbed gills that can be hard to see. The pores of this mushroom are covered with loose, white powder. If you cut into this mushroom, the flesh is all white.

Interestingly, the true color of the lobster mushroom is white, and the slightly hard red-orange shell is formed by a moldy parasite (*Lobster Mushroom*, n.d.)! (Don't worry, it's all perfectly edible.)

Habitat

In the Midwest, you can find lobster mushrooms from July to October. Seek them out in mixed forests, often buried in debris beneath the trees. You don't have to travel far into the forest to find them; as you travel along walking trails, look for telltale bumps alongside the trail that might contain a lobster mushroom (*Lobster Mushroom*, n.d.).

How to Gather

You might need to dig a bit with a trowel, as these mushrooms can sink inside the ground, effectively hiding the stems. Cut the stem with your knife, and then give the cup a good shake and brush to clean away most of the dirt trapped in the cup.

How to Prepare

Take care to clean out the inside of the cup-shaped cap, which tends to trap a lot of dirt and debris. Use water to wash the dirt away, then cut away any parts that are still dirty. Afterward, they'll keep in your fridge for a few days if stored in a paper bag or other breathable storage container.

In the kitchen, you can treat this mushroom just as you'd treat crab or lobster meat. Cook it up simply in some butter, add it to various seafood dishes, or make some tasty seafood soup!

Nutritional Content/ Benefits

Lobster mushrooms are delicious and healthy, with tons of vitamin D, A, and C (Stephenson, 2018).

Lobster rolls are a classic New England dish, made more interesting by the use of mushrooms instead of the usual crustacean!

Spicy Lobster Mushroom Roll

Ingredients:

- 1 lb lobster mushrooms
- ¼ tsp paprika
- 1 clove minced garlic
- ¼ cup cooking oil
- 3 tbsp lemon juice
- ¼ tsp salt

- ⅛ tsp black pepper
- ½ cup chopped celery
- ⅓ cup mayonnaise
- ½ tsp hot sauce
- 4-6 rolls
- 2-3 tbsp butter

Instructions:

1. Heat oil in a pan over medium, then add lobster mushrooms. Cook, occasionally stirring, until the liquid dissipates and the mushrooms begin to brown.
2. Toss in the garlic, sprinkle the paprika and cook for 30 seconds until the garlic is fragrant.
3. Take the mushrooms off the heat and prepare the rolls. Slather them with butter and toast them on both sides in a pan.
4. Mix together the cooled mushrooms, lemon juice, salt, pepper, celery, mayonnaise, and hot sauce. Add the filling evenly to each toasted bun.
5. Serve and enjoy!

Adapted from (*Bergo*, n.d.-f).

WARNING

The lobster mushroom is entirely unique, with no close lookalikes so that amateurs can hunt their fill of them. However, always be sure to confirm the identity of any mushroom you forage.

Painted Slippery Cap (Suillus spraguei)

The painted slippery cap is the rare "slippery" mushroom that's not dripping with slime. Rather, it looks like a colorfully-painted piece of artwork that contrasts with the dark autumnal forest.

How to Identify

This crackly-cap mushroom features a dry, cracked, brick red layer that reveals a yellow skin underneath. This cap can be rounded or flat. Rather than gills, the underside resembles a yellow, porous sponge cake.

The stem has the same color pattern as the cap, a pale yellow covered with red fibrous scales. When the mushroom is young, the porous underside is covered by a white veil, which then pulls away to become a white-gray ring around the stem (*Painted Suillus*, 2018).

Habitat

Painted slippery caps can be found through the end of summer and fall. These mushrooms grow under easter white pines in coniferous forests in the middle to eastern-most parts of the Midwest, but no farther west than Minnesota (*Painted Suillus*, 2018).

How to Gather

Cut the stem to pluck away this mushroom.

How to Prepare

The red scales wash away with the rain so they may wash away with a good rinsing. You need to cut away the porous underside and possibly the upper layer of skin. Be aware that the cut flesh will turn a dark color, but it remains edible (*Suillus Spraguei: The Ultimate Mushroom Guide*, n.d.)!

The yellow flesh of this mushroom can be used in similar ways to other "slippery" mushrooms, fried or sauteed in some simple recipes, or added to soups and pasta dishes.

Nutritional Content/ Benefits

As one of the less-popular edible members of the slippery *Suillus* family, there is a lack of research about its nutritional benefits. However, as a mushroom, it provides plenty of minerals, vitamins, and benefits to those who eat it.

This famous soup is the perfect recipe to incorporate the meaty slippery painted mushroom—not to mention the perfect comforting fall meal.

Hungarian Mushroom Soup

Ingredients:

- 4 tbsp butter
- 2 cups chopped onions
- 1 lb sliced painted slippery cap mushrooms
- 2 cups vegetable stock
- ½ cup dry white wine
- 2 tsp dried dill
- 2 tsp thyme
- 2 tsp paprika
- 2 tbsp soy sauce
- 1 cup whole milk
- 3 tbsp flour
- ¼ cup sour cream
- 2 tbsp lemon juice
- 2 tbsp fresh Italian parsley

Instructions:

1. Melt the butter in a large soup pot on medium heat. Saute the onions and mushrooms for about 10 minutes until the onions are translucent and the mushrooms are soft.
2. Mix in the dill, thyme, paprika, broth, soy sauce, and white wine. Turn down the heat slightly, cover the pot, and let the soup simmer until it reduces, about 10 minutes. Be careful not to let the soup boil.
3. In a large bowl, pour in the milk. Slowly whisk in the flour. Once it's smooth, pour this mixture into the soup and mix well. Cook for another 10 minutes until the soup thickens.
4. Pour in sour cream and lemon juice, stirring well and letting the whole soup heat through. Then sprinkle in the parsley as a final touch.
5. Serve and enjoy!

Adapted from (*Hungarian Mushroom Soup*, n.d.).

WARNING

Even though the painted slippery cap has no toxic lookalikes, always confirm the identity of edible mushrooms you plan to eat.

Pinkmottle Woodwax
(Hygrophorus russula)

This little mushroom certainly earns the descriptor "mottled," as it's decorated with splashes of red, purple, and pink in random patterns. The pinkmottle woodwax mushroom slightly resembles an Easter egg that was dipped in three different dyes!

How to Identify

These mushrooms have rounded, flat, or cup-shaped caps with the coloring mentioned above, usually pink and white but with splashes of red and purple. As the "wax" in its name indicates, the cap has a waxy sheen.

The gills are white and pink, all the same length and running down to touch the top of the stem. The stem itself has the same coloring as the gills, mottled white and pink. It can grow fairly thick, sometimes bulbous, and as large as the cap.

Habitat

In this region, you can find pink-mottle woodwax in late summer and early autumn, usually in August and September. Look under hardwood trees in forests, meadows, and lawns all over the Midwest, particularly near oak trees (*Hygrophorus Russula: The Ultimate Mushroom Guide*, n.d.).

How to Gather

Cut thick stems or pinch and twist thinner stems to gather these mushrooms. Pick smaller, younger mushrooms with rounded caps, which will be more tender and edible.

How to Prepare

Clean out the gills and wipe off the cap. Slice up the young cap and use them in all the ways you would use a store-bought button mushroom. Bake them on pizza, toss them in a salad, add them to a stir-fry, or boil them in a stew. You can also pickle them as a crunchy snack (Bergo, n.d.-d).

Nutritional Content/ Benefits

More research is needed to determine the exact nutritional benefits of the pinkmottle woodwax. But as a mushroom, it offers lots of health benefits and nutrients.

Mild-tasting pinkmottle woodwax mushrooms can add texture and taste to many meals, including this julienne dish.

Pinkmottle Woodwax Julienne

Ingredients:

- ½ cup sliced pinkmottle
- 2 tbsp cooking oil
- 2-4 tbsp dry white wine
- ¼ cup diced yellow onion
- 2 diced garlic cloves
- 1 tbsp unsalted butter
- 2 tsp all-purpose flour
- ½ cup sour cream
- ¼ cup parmesan cheese
- ½ tsp thyme
- ¼ tsp nutmeg

Instructions:

1. Heat oil in a pan over medium heat, then add the pinkmottle slices. Cook them on both sides until they're browned and start to carmelize. Set the cooked mushrooms aside.
2. Add more oil to the pan. Cook the onion in the pan until it becomes translucent, and then add the garlic and cook for another 30 seconds—season with salt and pepper.
3. Mix the mushrooms into the onion and garlic, then mix in the butter. Coat all the pan contents with the melting butter, then mix in the flour. Once everything is coated in the flour, cook for another 2 minutes, then pour in the wine.
4. When the wine mostly dissipates, add the sour cream and cheese and mix well.
5. Pour the pan contents into a baking dish. Cook at 375F for 5 minutes, add more loose cheese to the top and then cook for 5 more minutes until the cheese on top browns lightly.
6. Let cool, then serve and enjoy!

Adapted from (*Bergo*, n.d.-a).

WARNING

This colorful mushroom has no poisonous lookalikes but always confirm its identity whenever you pick a mushroom you want to eat.

Purple-Gilled Laccaria
(Laccaria ochropurpurea)

Another colorful fungi you might spot in the Midwest is the purple-gilled russula, a lavender mushroom that brightens the landscape. It only has a mild taste, so if you'd rather pass it up in favor of other edible mushrooms, at least stop to take a picture!

How to Identify

The delightful purple-gilled laccaria has a rounded, flat, or cup-shaped cap that comes in shades of lavender and tan. With age, the cap might turn a white-gray color. The thick, spacious gills on the underside are usually lavender, no matter the color of the cap.

Its thick, club-like stem can bulge out towards either the bot-tom or top and is whitish-tan with hints of gray and lavender (*Purple-Gilled Laccaria*, n.d.).

Habitat

Purple-gilled laccarias appear from July to November. Search for them in almost all Midwestern habitats that feature hardwood or conifer trees. You can find these mushrooms alongside other edible mushrooms under eastern white pine trees, oak trees, and beech trees (*Purple-Gilled Laccaria*, n.d.).

How to Gather

Use your pocket knife to cut the thick stem. Brush the cap and gills to get rid of dirt and spread spores before putting them in your bag.

How to Prepare

You can separate the stem from the cap, as the cap is infinitely more edible. Either dry the caps or store them fresh for a few days.

Slice up or use the whole cap in a variety of dishes, just like you would use button mushrooms. You can sautee them, add them to pizzas or pasta, and even pickle them.

Nutritional Content/ Benefits

Although the exact health benefits of the purple-gilled russula remain unknown, it's a good bet that it provides benefits similar to other mushrooms, such as antioxidants and immune-boosting properties.

The mild taste of this mushroom can enhance any autumn casserole or stir-fry.

Purple Gilled Mushroom Casserole

Ingredients:

- ¼ cup olive oil
- 4 cups purple gilled laccaria caps
- 2 tsp salt
- 1 cup chopped onion
- 1 tbsp minced garlic cloves
- ½ tsp pepper
- ½ tsp thyme
- 1 cup shredded cheese

Instructions:

1. Heat the oil in a pan over medium heat. Toss in the mushroom caps and onions and cook them until the liquid dissipates and they begin to brown.
2. Sprinkle with salt, pepper, garlic, and thyme. Cook until the garlic is fragrant, about 30 seconds.
3. Scoop the mushrooms into a greased baking dish. Bake for 10 minutes on 400F. Sprinkle cheese over the top and continue baking for another 5-10 minutes until the cheese has melted.
4. Serve and enjoy!

Adapted from (*DeLeeuw*, 2020).

Toxic *Cortinarius* mushrooms might also feature purple gills, and you definitely don't want to eat these. These poisonous mushrooms have a cobweb of tissue near the top of the stem, which is absent on the edible purple-gilled laccaria (*Purple-Gilled Laccaria*, n.d.).

Cortinarius violaceus.

Resinous Polypore
(Ischnoderma resinosum)

Another shelf mushroom growing on Midwestern trees and logs is the resinous polypore. This mushroom is quite attractive, with beautiful colors and a fragrant anise-like smell.

How to Identify

The velvety shelf-like caps of the resinous polypore feature colorful bands of white, gray, and shades of brown. The outer edge and porous underside are both light, white or off-white. The underside darkens with age, however.

The caps usually have a semi-circular fan shape and can range in size, either thin or thick. There's no stem, but sometimes a bit of cap attaches this mushroom directly to the trees or logs where they grow (*Resinous Polypore*, n.d.).

Habitat

Hunt for resinous polypores in September and October, when the leaves begin to turn. They appear to be growing horizontally from deciduous logs, stumps, and dead or dying trees (*Resinous Polypore*, n.d.).

How to Gather

Seek out younger mushrooms with thick caps and a bit of amber-colored "resin" coating the pores. These mushrooms will be the best for cooking. Use your knife to cut the mushroom away from the tree or log.

How to Prepare

Cut away the most tender parts of the mushroom to use in your dish. Wipe away any dirty places, but don't submerge them in water since they might become waterlogged.

You can experiment with these mushrooms, frying them with flour or tossing them in a stir-fry. Cook them until the liquid inside evaporates, and they become browned and tender, ready to eat.

Nutritional Content/ Benefits

More research needs to be done on the exact health benefits of eating the resinous polypore, but like other mushrooms, it provides a plethora of vitamins and minerals.

This dish makes great use of the resinous polypore and is a delicious and warming meal perfect for the late autumn months.

Meatballs with Resinous Polypore Gravy

Ingredients:

- 1 lb small meatballs
- 1 cup fresh resinous polypores
- 2 cups beef stock
- ½ cup heavy cream
- 2 tbsp all-purpose flour

- 3 tbsp butter
- ¼ cup brandy
- ¼ tsp salt
- 1 tsp thyme
- 1 diced yellow onion

Instructions:

1. Melt the butter in a deep pan or pot over medium heat. Add the meatballs and brown them thoroughly, then remove.
2. Add the mushrooms to the same pan or pot and continue cooking them in the butter. Once the liquid dissipates, add the onion and cook until the onion becomes translucent and the mushrooms brown.
3. Add a bit more butter to coat the mushrooms and onion thoroughly, then add the flour. Make sure it coats everything in the pan, sticking with the butter. Splash in the brandy and cook for one more minute.
4. Pour in the stock once the brandy reduces and return the meatballs to the pan or pot. Add in the heavy cream. Turn the heat down to the lowest setting, and cook for 45 minutes, stirring occasionally.
5. Sprinkle the thyme in the gravy and meatballs.
6. Serve and enjoy!

WARNING

This mushroom is fairly safe for beginners to identify, with no toxic lookalikes. Always be careful when identifying the mushrooms you plan to eat, however.

Shrimp of the Woods
(Entoloma abortivum)

This mushroom is unique even in the world of fungi in that it has two forms: you might see a version that looks like a lump of pink-white flesh, or you might see a version that looks like just another white gilled mushroom. Be aware that in some Midwestern states, you can only gather this mushroom in its lumpy form!

How to Identify

The two forms of this mushroom are called "aborted" and "unaborted." The aborted form is produced when this fungus infects and takes over other mushrooms. It produces a lumpy white mass with pink and white flesh inside. This one can appear like a peeled shrimp at a glance.

The unaborted form features a rounded, flat, or cup-shaped cap and club-like stalk, all of which are a uniform gray-white color. The gills run down into the stem and start out gray but turn somewhat pink with age (Nelson & Walting, 2017).

Habitat

Catch some shrimp of the woods from late summer through the fall, from the middle of September to the end of October. You can find the lumpy shrimp of the woods near the habitat of honey mushrooms, usually on the forest floor on top of decaying leaves or wood (Nelson & Walting, 2017).

How to Gather

If you're foraging in Michigan, be aware that you can only gather the lumpy aborted form. In other states, you can gather both, but it's advised that you only pick the lumpy version, which is much easier to identify and eat.

Pick the small, white, lumpy mushrooms, and check them for bugs. Carefully pluck up and cut away any of these mushrooms you find, and brush them off as well as you can before putting them in your bag (*Entoloma Abortivum – Midwest American Mycological Information*, n.d.).

How to Prepare

Clean the mushroom off as best as you can before cooking it, as dirt is easily trapped in the knobbly form of the mushroom. These mushrooms will last a few days in your fridge when stored in an open, breathable container.

Afterward, you can use these mushrooms in dozens of recipes, especially dishes that call for shrimp. Add them to seafood bakes, fry them up, toss them on the barbeque, make delicious shrimp of the woods tacos, or serve them up with some yummy dip (*Good Natured: Shrimp of The Woods! You Can Barbecue It, Boil It, Broil It, Bake It …*, 2021).

Nutritional Content/ Benefits

There is a lack of research on the health benefits of this mushroom, but all edible mushrooms contain healthy vitamins and minerals that benefit the humans who eat them!

RECIPE/REMEDY

Shrimp of the woods not only looks like a peeled shrimp but also tastes like one (*Good Natured: Shrimp of The Woods! You Can Barbecue It, Boil It, Broil It, Bake It ...*, 2021)!

Shrimp of the Woods Scampi Pasta

Ingredients:

- 8 oz fettuccine
- 1 tbsp olive oil
- 1 tbsp unsalted butter
- 2.5 cups sliced shrimps of the woods mushrooms
- ¼ tsp salt
- ⅛ tsp pepper

- ½ cup chopped white onion
- 4 minced garlic cloves
- ½ cup vegetable stock
- 4 tbsp unsalted butter
- ½ tsp salt
- ¼ tsp black pepper

Instructions:

1. Boil the pasta in a pot of water on the stove.
2. In a pan over medium heat, heat the oil and butter. Add the onions. Season them with salt and pepper. Saute them until they become translucent.
3. Add the mushrooms to the pan and cook them until they are mostly soft. Then add the garlic and cook for about 30 seconds, until fragrant.
4. Pour in the stock and stir, letting the contents of the pan simmer for 3-4 minutes. Melt in the last bit of butter, season with salt and pepper, and continue to heat and stir until the butter incorporates into the dish!
5. Pour the sauce over the cooked and drained pasta.
6. Serve and enjoy!

Adapted from (*Garlic Butter Mushroom Shrimp Pasta Recipe*, 2018).

The lumpy form of the shrimp of the woods has no toxic lookalikes; it's truly unique in the world of fungi and an excellent target for beginners! Avoid the unaborted form, which is almost indistinguishable from poisonous *Amanita* mushrooms (*Entoloma Abortivum – Midwest American Mycological Information*, n.d.). Stay safe and always double-check the identity of any mushroom you pick.

Wood Blewit (Clitocybe nuda)

Autumn foragers have the chance to spot lots of colorful mushrooms in the forests and lawns of the Midwest, including the breathtaking wood blewit. When you find this mushroom, spend a moment taking in its breathtaking colors before you take it home and fry it up!

How to Identify

Wood blewit caps are bright autumn-leaf brown, but the edges are tinged with lilac purple. The caps are rounded. The gills are also lilac, with hints of brown, while the stem is brown and white. There will be a gap between the gills and stem.

Habitat

These fall mushrooms appear in October and last through December, depending on the weather.

Find them in Midwestern mixed forests, growing from the littered forest floor. On your autumn hikes, glance at the floor around oak trees to spot hints of purple (Shaw, 2020).

How to Gather

Find small, young mushrooms and pull them up by twisting the stem.

How to Prepare

You can eat the whole cap, so clean the gills and rinse off the cap. This mushroom can easily be dried, refrigerated, or used in dishes. Experiment with methods of cooking—sauteing with butter, frying them in flour, or pickled as a delicious chewy snack (Shaw, 2020).

Nutritional Content/Benefits

Wood blewits can provide thiamin, a nutrient that supports your nervous system. It has few calories and no harmful cholesterol (*The Wood Blewit Mushroom: Clitocybe Nuda & Lepista Nuda Benefits*, 2021).

RECIPE/REMEDY

Mild-tasting, slightly chewy wood blewits aren't exactly the superstars of the culinary mushroom world, but they can still be a tasty addition to many warm autumn dishes.

Wild Mushroom Ragout

Ingredients:

- 1.5 lb wood blewits
- 4 tbsp butter
- 2 sliced leeks
- 2 cloves minced garlic
- ¼ tsp salt
- ¼ tsp thyme
- 1 bay leaf
- ⅛ tsp cayenne pepper
- ⅛ tsp crushed red pepper flakes
- ¼ cup dry white wine
- ½ cup vegetable stock
- ½ cup creme fraiche

Instructions:

1. In a deep pan on the stove, melt the butter. Add the wood blewits and cook them for a few minutes.
2. Season the mushrooms with salt, thyme, cayenne pepper, and pepper flakes, then add the leeks and garlic. Cook for about 30 seconds until the garlic is fragrant.
3. Splash the wine, and let the wine reduce before adding in the vegetable stock. Turn up the heat slightly and simmer the broth until it heats through and reduces.
4. Test that the mushrooms have turned thoroughly soft. Mix in the creme fraiche and make sure everything is heated before you take the ragout off the stove.
5. Serve and enjoy!

Adapted from (*Wild Mushroom Ragout | Love and Olive Oil*, 2018).

A purple mushroom you find might be the wood blewit, or it might be a toxic *Cortinarius*. Look closely at the spore print and upper stem to determine which you have; the Cortinarius has some cobweb-like tissue near the top of the stem, and its spore print is dark red. The edible wood blewit lacks this cobwebbing and has a light pink spore print (Shaw, 2020).

Cortinarius violaceus.

Other Books You'll Love

Conclusion

The vast, sprawling region of the Midwest is infinitely explorable for the intrepid forager. Whether you live in America's heartland or are simply traveling there on a foraging trip, you can spend days foraging in most regions and seasons and never run out of mushrooms to unearth and eat.

No matter your previous foraging experience or your target mushroom or habitat, you can use this book to guide you in searching out and positively identifying edible mushrooms in the wild. If you're a beginner, pick one of the more easily-identifiable mushrooms and start there. For experienced foragers, seek out some mushrooms you've overlooked or never found before!

This book provides wisdom from mushroom experts and plenty of tried-and-tested advice about distinguishing delicious, edible mushrooms from the deceitful, toxic varieties. Take this book with you, along with other seasoned foragers, into the field. Always remember never to trust a mushroom at first sight—double-check and closely observe all the mushroom's features, comparing them against the information found here to confirm its identity. The number one rule of mushroom hunting is staying safe!

Once you get your mushrooms home, use the recipes in this book to cook up any number of recipes. Share them with your friends and family, especially if you've found a giant puffball, and don't be afraid to experiment with your harvest! Try new recipes and share them with your fellow foragers and mycology clubs. Foraging can be fun on its own, but it's even more fun when it's shared with others.

Now that you've learned all about these fascinating, appetizing fungi from the pages of this book, you can venture into the forests, highlands, and prairies of the Midwest and discover all the shining oyster mushrooms, vibrant chanterelles, slimy, slippery caps, and juicy milk caps that your heart desires!

What are you waiting for? It's time to hit the trail or park path and start your Midwestern foraging adventure!